The Mystery

MW00527465

The Messiahship of Jesus in the Qur'an, New Testament, Old Testament, and Other Sources

Louay Fatoohi

Luna Plena Publishing   Birmingham

© 2009 Louay Fatoohi

All Rights reserved. No part of this book may be reproduced, translated, stored in a retrieval system, or transmitted by any means, electronic, mechanical, photocopying, recording, or otherwise, without written permission from the author.

Scripture quotations are from The Holy Bible, English Standard Version®, copyright © 2001 by Crossway Bibles, a publishing ministry of Good News Publishers. Used by permission. All rights reserved.

First published: May 2009

Production Reference: 1010509

Published by:
Luna Plena Publishing
Birmingham, UK.
www.lunaplenapub.com

ISBN 978-1-906342-05-0

Cover design by:
Mawlid Design
www.mawliddesign.com

Cover image:
The image on the front cover shows the characteristic attributes of the Messiah in Judaism, Christianity, and Islam. The crown symbolizes the Jewish Messiah as the heir of King David, the suffering Christian Messiah is represented by the cross, and the Muslim Messiah is described in this Qur'anic verse:

The Messiah son of Mary was no other than a messenger before whom [similar] messengers passed away, and his mother was a saintly woman. They used to eat food [like other human beings]. See how We make the revelations clear to them, and see how they are deluded! (5.75)

About the Author

Louay Fatoohi is a British scholar who was born in Baghdad, Iraq, in 1961. He converted from Christianity to Islam in his early twenties. He obtained a BSc in Physics from the College of Sciences, University of Baghdad, in 1984. He obtained his PhD in Astronomy from the Physics Department, Durham University, in 1998.

The author of several books and over forty scientific and general articles in Arabic and English, Dr Fatoohi is particularly interested in studying historical characters and events that are mentioned in the Qur'an and comparing the Qur'anic account with the Biblical narratives, other Jewish and Christian writings, and historical sources. His most recent books are:

- *The Mystery of the Crucifixion: The Attempt to Kill Jesus in the Qur'an, the New Testament, and Historical Sources.*

- *The Mystery of Israel in Ancient Egypt: The Exodus in the Qur'an, the Old Testament, Archaeological Finds, and Historical Sources.*

- *The Mystery of the Historical Jesus: The Messiah in the Qur'an, the Bible, and Historical Sources.*

- *The Prophet Joseph in the Qur'an, the Bible, and History: A new detailed commentary on the Qur'anic Chapter of Joseph.*

The knowledge of any person is determined only partly by what they know and more by what they do not

Contents

Preface

My book *The Mystery of the Historical Jesus: The Messiah in the Qur'an, the Bible, and Historical Sources* is a comprehensive study of all aspects of Jesus' life and teachings. It was always my intention to use parts of that work as the core for smaller, more focused books each of which covers certain aspects of the life of Jesus in more detail. I have already published a book on the crucifixion, and this is the second of these derivative works.

This book is based mainly on the chapter on the Messiah and content from other chapters in my book on the historical Jesus. The study has been significantly expanded with new material. The presentation of the reused content has also been substantially changed and improved.

This book continues the effort of my previous writings to achieve two related goals. **First**, to bring the Qur'an to a study field that Western scholarship has restricted to the Old and New Testaments and historical writings. **Second**, to get Islamic studies of the Qur'an to extend their scope to include historical sources and to also look more closely at the Old and New Testaments and other Jewish and Christian sources.

In this book, I focus on the concept of "Messiah" in the Qur'an, the Bible, and Dead Sea Scrolls. While history has played a significant part in how the image of the "Messiah" has changed over time and that history needs to be cited, this religious concept is dealt with almost exclusively in religious, even though not necessarily scriptural, sources. Independent historical sources do not help much when studying this concept.

All my writings have benefits greatly from the insightful comments and feedback of my wife Shetha Al-Dargazelli. Shetha's support has also played a major role in enabling me to write my books.

The comments of my close friend Tariq Chaudhry have also allowed me to improve the book significantly.

Introduction

The Messiah is the main figure in Christianity, as this religion was formed around Jesus' messiahship. Judaism also gives the Messiah a special position, although it denies that Jesus was the Messiah, so the Jews continue to wait for the coming of their Messiah.

The Qur'an confirms the Christian belief that Jesus was the Messiah, but it has fundamental differences with the Christian representation of the Messiah. It has even more differences with the Jewish concept of the Messiah.

In this book, I will compare the concept of "Messiah" in Judaism, Christianity, and Islam, focusing on the Qur'an in the latter case. I will try and develop a complete picture of how this concept appeared, what it originally represented, and how it was changed over time. My ultimate goal is to show that the Qur'anic Messiah is the historical one, and that both the Jewish and Christian Messiahs were developed greatly by followers of these religions.

The book consists of 12 chapters and 1 appendix. **Chapter 1** examines in detail the concept of "Messiah" in the Old Testament and other Jewish literature, including the Dead Sea Scrolls. The Messiah in Christianity is the subject of **Chapter 2**. Introducing the concept of the "Messiah" in the three religions that embrace it is completed in **Chapter 3** by studying this concept in the Qur'an.

Chapters 4-10 each discusses one element of the image of the Messiah in Christianity and Judaism and then compares it with the Qur'an. **Chapter 4** focuses on whether Jesus declared publicly that he was the awaited Messiah. The Jewish and Christian claim that the Messiah was the king of the Jews is then examined in **Chapter 5**.

The fact that the Christian Messiah did not establish his expected kingdom has led to the belief that he will return. Jesus' "second coming" is studied in **Chapter 6**. The question whether or not Jesus was a "son of David" is answered in **Chapter 7**. **Chapter 8** then scrutinizes the claim of Jewish and Christian sources that the Messiah had a unique salvational role.

Both the Qur'an and the Gospels present Jesus as an exceptional miracle worker. This is the subject of **Chapter 9**. Christianity differs from Judaism and Islam in presenting its Messiah as someone who suffered on behalf of people. This difference is discussed in **Chapter 10**.

Following in the footsteps of the Gospel writers, Christians have always been interested in presenting Old Testament prophecies as having been fulfilled in Jesus. This approach is critically examined in **Chapter 11**. Finally, **Chapter 12** summarizes the findings of the previous 11 chapters as it draws the image of the historical Messiah.

For reference, all Qur'anic verses in which the term "Messiah" occurs have been compiled in **Appendix A**.

For the reader's convenience, the book has three indexes for the Qur'anic verses, Biblical passages, and general names and subjects.

The book uses a number of styles. Each Qur'anic verse has been followed by a combination of two numbers identifying its *sūra* or "chapter" and its position in that chapter. For instance, the combination 4.172 refers to the 172nd verse of the 4th chapter.

The translations of the Qur'an in the book are mine, even though I have consulted some English translations. As translation is an act of interpretation, reflecting the translator's understanding of the text, I always use my own translations of the Qur'an.

Square brackets have been used to enclose explanatory texts that are needed to clarify the translation. Alternative texts, such as the English meaning of a term that is quoted in its Arabic origin, are enclosed in parentheses.

For Biblical quotes, I have used the *English Standard Version* (ESV) Bible. First published in 2001, this modern translation is partly based on the *King James Version*.

The book uses a number of different printing styles. Different fonts have been used for the text, Qur'anic verses, and Biblical passages. Roman transliterations of Arabic terms are in italics.

Finally, I welcome any feedback from readers at the following email address   fatoohi_louay@gmail.com   or   through   my   website www.quranicstudies.com.

1

Messiahship in Judaism

The title "Messiah," which is *Mashiaḥ* in Hebrew and *Meshiḥa* in Aramaic, means the "anointed one." It is derived from the religious practice of pouring oil on an anointed object or the head of a person. Anointment was used to sanctify or dedicate things to God, such as consecrating an altar (Exo. 29:36). For human beings, anointment is used as hygienic practice. But the kind of anointment that concerns us here is the practice that denoted God's support for and approval of the anointed person for a particular mission or position of leadership.

There are a number of fundamental facts that encompass the use and development of the title "Messiah" in Judaism. **First**, in the Old Testament, this title is not applied to only one person or role, but it is used for a number of different people and positions. All these "Messiahs" are *historical* figures from Jewish history. The Jewish scripture applies this term to men who lived in the past.

Second, while the Old Testament talks about *future* individuals who would play salvational roles in Israel's history, the title "Messiah" is never used for or associated with any of these saviors.

Third, later political upheavals in Jewish history resulted in the association of the title "Messiah" with a liberator who would gather the dispersed Israelites in Palestine and restore their kingdom. This savior was also made *eschatological*, i.e. coming at the end of times. Scriptural passages that might have referred to different salvational individuals started to be seen as talking about that one savior. While giving this figure a salvational role and making him appear at the end of times were human ideas that appeared in response to certain human needs, the concept of one important future figure called "Messiah" was old and divinely inspired. The image of this historical "one Messiah" was changed to meet the salvational and eschatological needs of Israel.

Fourth, some Jewish groups believed in more than one eschatological Messiah.

These major facts are the focus of this chapter.

Historical Messiahs in the Old Testament

In its 39 occurrences in the Old Testament, the term "Messiah" is applied to certain individuals who occupied three different positions: king, priest, and prophet. It is also used for the nation of Israel. Let's look at some passages that mention the anointment of individuals who occupied such positions:

(1) **Kings**: The Old Testament says that prophet Samuel anointed Saul as king:

> Then Samuel took a flask of oil and poured it on his head and kissed him and said, "Has not the Lord anointed you to be prince over his people Israel? And you shall reign over the people of the Lord and you will save them from the hand of their surrounding enemies. And this shall be the sign to you that the Lord has anointed you to be prince over his heritage." (1 Sam. 10:1)

After God's rejection of Saul from being king over Israel, He commanded Samuel to anoint a new king and sent him to a Bethlehemite called Jesse to find the new king among his sons. Samuel could not recognize the future king in any of Jesse's seven sons that were presented to him, so he asked Jesse to bring his youngest son, David — the only one who had not been presented to Samuel:

> And he sent and brought him in. Now he was ruddy and had beautiful eyes and was handsome. And the Lord said, "Arise, anoint him, for this is he." Then Samuel took the horn of oil and anointed him in the midst of his brothers. And the Spirit of the Lord rushed upon David from that day forward. (1 Sam. 16:12-13)

David's son and his successor as king, Solomon, also described himself as an "anointed one" in this prayer:

> O Lord God, do not turn away the face of your anointed one! Remember your steadfast love for David your servant. (2 Chr. 6:42)

(2) **Priests**: In this passage God speaks to Moses about the anointment of his brother Aaron and his sons as priests:

> Then you shall bring Aaron and his sons to the entrance of the tent of meeting and shall wash them with water and put on Aaron the holy garments. And you shall anoint him and consecrate him, that he may serve me as priest. You shall bring his sons also and put coats on them, and anoint them, as you anointed their father, that they may serve me as priests. And their anointing shall admit them to a perpetual priesthood throughout their generations. (Exo. 40:12-15)

This is another passage in which God speaks to Moses about the anointed high priests:

If it is the anointed priest who sins, thus bringing guilt on the people, then he shall offer for the sin that he has committed a bull from the herd without blemish to the Lord for a sin offering. He shall bring the bull to the entrance of the tent of meeting before the Lord and lay his hand on the head of the bull and kill the bull before the Lord. And the anointed priest shall take some of the blood of the bull and bring it into the tent of meeting. (Lev. 4:3-5)

This pericope talks about anointing a king and a priest:

And they ate and drank before the Lord on that day with great gladness. And they made Solomon the son of David king the second time, and they anointed him as prince for the Lord, and Zadok as priest. (1 Chr. 29:22)

(3) Prophets: One example of the anointment of an unnamed prophet is found in this passage:

The Spirit of the Lord God is upon me, because the Lord has anointed me to bring good news to the poor; he has sent me to bind up the brokenhearted, to proclaim liberty to the captives, and the opening of the prison to those who are bound. (Isa. 61:1)

God's following words to prophet Elijah mention the anointment of two kings and a prophet:

Go, return on your way to the wilderness of Damascus. And when you arrive, you shall anoint Hazael to be king over Syria. And Jehu the son of Nimshi you shall anoint to be king over Israel, and Elisha the son of Shaphat of Abel-meholah you shall anoint to be prophet in your place. (1 Kings 19:15-16)

(4) Israel: The Old Testament uses the term "Messiah" as a referent for the entire people of Israel also. The following prayer, which mentions God's promise to Abraham, is attributed to King David:

Remember his covenant forever, the word that he commanded, for a thousand generations, the covenant that he made with Abraham, his sworn promise to Isaac, which he confirmed as a statute to Jacob, as an everlasting covenant to Israel, saying, "To you I will give the land of Canaan, as your portion for an inheritance." When you were few in number, and of little account, and sojourners in it, wandering from nation to nation, from one kingdom to another people, he allowed no one to oppress them; he rebuked kings on their account, saying, "Touch not my anointed ones, do my prophets no harm!" (1 Chr. 16:15-22)

This prayer appears also in Psalm 105 (8-15).

So the Old Testament applies the title "anointed" to kings, priests, prophets, and Israel. But it does not restrict this title to Israelites. It applies it also to the Persian king Cyrus (580/590-529 BCE):

> Thus says the Lord to his anointed, to Cyrus, whose right hand I have grasped, to subdue nations before him and to loose the belts of kings, to open doors before him that gates may not be closed. (Isa. 45:1)

After defeating the Babylonians in 539 BCE, Cyrus allowed the Jews, who had been taken captive from Jerusalem and forced into exile by the Babylonian king Nebuchadnezzar II early in that century, to go back to Palestine. The application of the term "anointed" to Cyrus is probably the result of seeing him as a key player in the divine plan to set the Jews free and send them back to their homeland.

There is one particularly important observation to stress: none of the figures that the Old Testament calls "Messiah" were associated with any future let alone eschatological expectations. They were "historical" Messiahs who lived in the past and had no function in the future.

Future Saviors in the Old Testament

The Old Testament contains a number of prophecies about future figures who would come to rescue Israel and defeat its enemy. There are three attributes common to *all* those figures. **First**, they are described as kings. **Second**, they are descendants of David. There are good reasons why these saviors are presented as Davidic kings. David was the king who established in the holy land the kingdom of the people of Israel. After the death of his son and successor Solomon around 930 BCE, the kingdom split into the northern kingdom of Israel and the southern kingdom of Judah or Judea. This split is seen as a major reason for the Israelites' subsequent loss of sovereignty and destitution, as Israel and Judea were later attacked and destroyed by the Assyrians and the Babylonians, respectively, and had their populations taken into exile. No salvational king would symbolize what the devastated Israelites needed and missed more than one from the offspring of the founder of the Israelite kingdom.

Secularists or, in general, those who do not consider these predictions as divine prophecies see them as manifestations of wishful thinking of the suffering Jews of the time. The prophets uttered what people were hoping and praying for.

Third, like their father, these salvational kings will be righteous, returning the Israelites to the way God had chosen for His people. Israel's desolation was the result of its sins and failure to follow God's commandments. Each of these passages predicts and promises the coming of a righteous salvational Davidic king:

Behold, the days are coming, declares the Lord, when I will raise up for David a righteous Branch, and he shall reign as king and deal wisely, and shall execute justice and righteousness in the land. In his days Judah will be saved, and Israel will dwell securely. And this is the name by which he will be called: "The Lord is our righteousness." (Jer. 23:5-6)

Thus says the Lord God: "Behold, I will take the people of Israel from the nations among which they have gone, and will gather them from all around, and bring them to their own land. And I will make them one nation in the land, on the mountains of Israel. And one king shall be king over them all, and they shall be no longer two nations, and no longer divided into two kingdoms. They shall not defile themselves anymore with their idols and their detestable things, or with any of their transgressions. But I will save them from all the backslidings in which they have sinned, and will cleanse them; and they shall be my people, and I will be their God. "My servant David shall be king over them, and they shall all have one shepherd. They shall walk in my rules and be careful to obey my statutes. They shall dwell in the land that I gave to my servant Jacob, where your fathers lived. They and their children and their children's children shall dwell there forever, and David my servant shall be their prince forever. I will make a covenant of peace with them. It shall be an everlasting covenant with them. And I will set them in their land and multiply them, and will set my sanctuary in their midst forevermore. My dwelling place shall be with them, and I will be their God, and they shall be my people. Then the nations will know that I am the Lord who sanctifies Israel, when my sanctuary is in their midst forevermore." (Eze. 37:21-28)

For to us a child is born, to us a son is given; and the government shall be upon his shoulder, and his name shall be called Wonderful Counselor, Mighty God, Everlasting Father, Prince of Peace. Of the increase of his government and of peace there will be no end, on the throne of David and over his kingdom, to establish it and to uphold it with justice and with righteousness from this time forth and forevermore. The zeal of the Lord of hosts will do this. (Isa. 9:6-7)

Note how the royal saviors are symbolically represented by David the founder of Israel.

The prophecies by Isaiah, Jeremiah, and Ezekiel were clearly influenced by the destruction of Israel on the hands of the Assyrians in the 7th century BCE and of Judea by the Babylonians in the following century.

The prophesied king will create a new world order in which Israel will live justly as God commanded it and which is just for all and free of any inequity:

There shall come forth a shoot from the stump of Jesse, and a branch from his roots shall bear fruit. And the Spirit of the Lord shall rest upon

him, the Spirit of wisdom and understanding, the Spirit of counsel and
might, the Spirit of knowledge and the fear of the Lord. And his delight
shall be in the fear of the Lord. He shall not judge by what his eyes see,
or decide disputes by what his ears hear, but with righteousness he shall
judge the poor, and decide with equity for the meek of the earth; and he
shall strike the earth with the rod of his mouth, and with the breath of his
lips he shall kill the wicked. Righteousness shall be the belt of his waist,
and faithfulness the belt of his loins. The wolf shall dwell with the lamb,
and the leopard shall lie down with the young goat, and the calf and the
lion and the fattened calf together; and a little child shall lead them. The
cow and the bear shall graze; their young shall lie down together; and the
lion shall eat straw like the ox. The nursing child shall play over the hole
of the cobra, and the weaned child shall put his hand on the adder's den.
They shall not hurt or destroy in all my holy mountain; for the earth shall
be full of the knowledge of the Lord as the waters cover the sea. In that
day the root of Jesse, who shall stand as a signal for the peoples — of
him shall the nations inquire, and his resting place shall be glorious. In
that day the Lord will extend his hand yet a second time to recover the
remnant that remains of his people, from Assyria, from Egypt, from
Pathros, from Cush, from Elam, from Shinar, from Hamath, and from the
coastlands of the sea. He will raise a signal for the nations and will
assemble the banished of Israel, and gather the dispersed of Judah from
the four corners of the earth. (Isa. 11:1-12)

Jesse is David's father. Note the use of the term "branch" by both
Jeremiah (23:5) and Isaiah (11:1). This term is used also by prophet
Zechariah (3:8) who quotes a prophecy in which God promises the
following to the high priest Joshua: "I will bring my servant the Branch."
But Zechariah uses the term "branch" as a reference to the then governor
of Judea, Zerubbabel. The referent is made absolutely clear in another
passage (Zech. 6:12).

This righteous kingdom will last forever, as in God's following
promise to David, conveyed to him by prophet Nathan, and in Psalm 89:

When your days are fulfilled to walk with your fathers, I will raise up
your offspring after you, one of your own sons, and I will establish his
kingdom. He shall build a house for me, and I will establish his throne
forever. I will be to him a father, and he shall be to me a son. I will not
take my steadfast love from him, as I took it from him who was before
you, but I will confirm him in my house and in my kingdom forever, and
his throne shall be established forever. (1 Chr. 17:11-14)

I have made a covenant with my chosen one; I have sworn to David my
servant: "I will establish your offspring forever, and build your throne for
all generations." (Ps. 89:3-4)

We saw in the last section that those who are called Messiahs are not associated with soteriological expectations, as they were historical not future individuals. An equally significant observation is that the prophetic passages above do not refer to any of their salvational figures with the term "Messiah." These Old Testament texts started to be spoken of as "messianic" prophecies or expectations only after the saviors they talk about started to be all seen as representing *one anointed* eschatological figure whose coming would usher a new world order.

The Future Saviors Become One Eschatological Messiah

While the term Messiah is applied in the Old Testament to *historical* not *future* figures, this started to change in later Jewish theology and literature. According to the *Jewish Encyclopedia*:

> "The Messiah" (with the article and not in opposition with another word) is, however, not an Old Testament expression, but occurs for the first time in apocalyptic literature. Similarly, in all probability, the use of the word "Mashiakh" to denote the Messianic king is not found earlier than the apocalyptic literature.

Scholars believe that after the overthrowing of the last Davidic ruler of Judea, Zedekiah, by Nebuchadnezzar II in 586 BCE, the concept of "anointed king" started to be understood to mean "*the* Messiah" — the final Jewish king who would free them from foreign control, reestablish the Jewish kingdom, and return to Israel its lost glory (Vermes, 2000: 177). The Jews started to give more attention to the figure of a Messiah particularly after the fall of the Maccabean dynasty (165-63 BCE), coming under Roman rule, and the usurping of Judea by Herod the Great (40-4 BCE) and his family who were backed by the heathen Romans. This waiting for the Messiah grew stronger in the years leading to the two Jewish revolts against the Roman in 66-70 and 132-135 CE. The several salvational Davidic figures started to be seen as one eschatological savior: "The Messiah." The prominence of the Messiah in the Jewish faith grew to the extent that the influential Jewish theologian and philosopher Maimonides (1135-1204 CE) made the belief in the Messiah and waiting for his coming the 12th of his 13 principles of Jewish faith.

One famous pretender to the role of the eschatological Messiah was Simon bar Kokhba who led a mutiny against Rome in 132 CE. The independent Jewish state that he founded lasted for three years only before Judea was reclaimed by the Romans and bar Kokhba was killed.

Some apologists argue that the non-use of the term "Messiah" in the Old Testament for a future savior does not indicate the absence of the concept of one and unique Messiah from that book. They maintain that it only reflects the fact that the technical designation for this concept was not formalized until later after the return of the exiled Jews from Babylon. This explanation lacks credibility for two reasons. **First**, it is difficult to see how the powerful and influential concept of such a unique future salvational figure could have existed without a specific title assigned to that figure. **Second**, the term "Messiah" was already used in the Old Testament for historical, less important figures, so if the Biblical authors had intended to write about the concept of *the Messiah* they would have used the term "Messiah" and it would not have had to wait for centuries before it is applied to that concept. The Biblical writers were either unaware of the concept of *the Messiah* or did not believe in it.

The Jewish interest in interpreting Biblical passages as being Messianic grew not only as a result of their blighted history and the need they felt for such a savior. It was also influenced by the keenness of Christians on seeing references to the Messiah, whom they believed was Jesus, in various Biblical passages. As put by one scholar:

> Far from the New Testament reflecting the views of contemporary Jewry, it is far more probable that many of the rabbinic views about the Messiah are, positively and negatively, the result of the impact of Christian teaching. (Ellison, 1953)

Those early Christian converts were Jews who, like other Jews, believed in the coming of the Messiah. Having accepted Jesus' claim to messiahship, they tried to convince their fellow Jews that the Messiah has come. They reckoned that the best way of doing that is by showing that Old Testament prophecies applied to Jesus. This did not manage to convince many Jews because hardly any of these alleged prophecies applied perfectly to Jesus. Later in the book, we will come across some supposed Biblical "prophecies" that Christians linked to Jesus. Chapter 11 focuses on examining some of these prophecies. But the attempt itself to use those Biblical passages must have had its effect in enforcing the perception that they were messianic.

But even during the unpleasant periods of Jewish history, the concept of the Messiah and messianic expectation were never central to Jewish theology:

> Christians with no expert knowledge of Jewish religious history tend to conceive of the Messiah as the central figure in the theology of the Jews in the ages of Jesus, a figure dominating every other hope of Judaism. In fact messianic fervour, far from being all-pervasive, was only sporadically attested in Jewish literature, mostly amid the political upheavals of the last two pre-Christian centuries and in the first century AD. The main messianic theme refers to the triumph of the future anointed king of the house of David, who was to restore the sovereignty of the Jewish people

after bringing to an end centuries of foreign domination and overthrowing the mighty Roman empire. (Vermes, 2000: 28-29)

This Christian overestimation of the position of *the Messiah* in Judaism is understandable given that Christianity was founded on and around the Messiah.

Associating Old Testament passages with the concept of an eschatological Messiah was not universal among the Jews.

The Divine Revelation about *the Messiah*

So the consensus among scholars is that a long troubled Jewish history lies behind the development of the concept of one salvational, eschatological Messiah. But serving the need for freedom of an oppressed nation abandoned temporarily by God to its enemies would not have required necessarily *one* savior or for him to be called *Messiah*. Any number of saviors would have done. Also, these saviors could have been given any titles and would not have needed to be called "Messiah." It may be argued that this title was used because anointment was a sign of acceptance and support by God, but then the very function associated with the figure in question *presumes* this divine support anyway, so there was no *necessity* for him to be anointed and thus called "Messiah." Where did the concept of *the Messiah*, i.e. *one Messiah*, come from then?

I find a clue to the answer to this question in the fact that the Qur'an talks about only *one Messiah*. Of course, Christian writings also focus on *one Messiah*. But it may be argued that the New Testament copied from the Jewish Messiah a big part of the image of its Christ, so the concept of *the Messiah* could also have been borrowed. Indeed, the Christian Messiah inherited attributes that were given to him by Judaism, such us being a savior and a king, even though Christianity was forced by the history of Jesus to redefine what these attributes actually meant. For instance, the Messiah's kingdom was made to be spiritual rather than earthly, because that is what Jesus preached.

But no such influence is seen on the Qur'anic Messiah who shares very little with the Christian Messiah and even less with his Jewish counterpart. The Qur'an speaks of one Messiah who had been expected by the time Jesus was born, but who is very different from the Messiah who is still being expected by the Jews or the one presented in Christian sources. Apart from identifying the Messiah with Jesus and presenting him as a miracle worker, the Qur'anic Messiah shares none of the attributes of the Christian Messiah. Those who do not believe in the divine origin of the Qur'an and, accordingly, think it was inspired by

Jewish and Christian literature and influence, would have to give a convincing explanation for this rather unnecessarily strange and different Messiah.

The unique Qur'anic Messiah leads me to conclude that the concept of *the Messiah* is of divine origin, having been inspired to prophets who were sent to the people of Israel. But human intervention distorted this concept over the centuries. Influenced by their troubled history, national aspirations, and misunderstanding of what it meant to be God's chosen people, Jewish theologians and writers developed a Jewish-centric image of the Messiah. This image was held by those who later became the first Christians, but after accepting that Jesus was the Messiah they had to redraw some of its details to reflect the history of Jesus. The image of the Messiah in Christian writings is based on what the Christians believed Jesus *actually* did and said, combined with some *expectations* about the future, so it differs from the portrait of the Jewish Messiah. The Qur'anic Messiah differs from the Jewish and Christian Messiahs, being presented as a highly elevated prophet of God. The Qur'an has preserved the concept of this unique Messiah as it was originally revealed to Israelite prophets, in contrast to the changed versions found in Jewish and Christian sources.

But if the concept of one future Messiah was inspired by God, why is it missing from the Old Testament? In fact, the term Messiah is not even applied to any future figure. There are two possible explanations for this omission. **First**, the coming of the future Messiah had not been revealed by the time the Old Testament was written. There is disagreement between scholars about which book of the Old Testament was written last. One traditional candidate is Malachi, which is thought to have been written around 450-500 BCE. A competing view considers Daniel as the last book and dates its writing to around 160 BCE. If the concept of a future Messiah appeared later than the last book, then it is natural not to be found in the Old Testament.

The **second** scenario is that the prophecy about a future Messiah was not as central as the later Jews and the Christians came to believe, so it was easy for it to get lost in the heavy editorial work that the Jewish scriptures went through. This prophecy was about a future prophet who, as a religious reformer, would come to rectify the distorted and wrong teachings that crept into Judaism over the centuries. In comparison with the concept of a national savior that developed later, this reformist Messiah was not particularly appealing to a humiliated nation looking for salvation from occupying forces, so it did not survive the time. Some Old Testament prophecies might have developed from the original revelation about the Messiah, but after being adapted to meet the national aspirations of the Jewish nation.

I find this second scenario more plausible, as it may explain the origin of some Old Testament prophecies about future saviors.

As to the presentation of this Messiah as eschatological, i.e. coming at the end of times, I think this is derived from a combination of recognizing him as "one," seeing him as a savior, and the need of the Jewish nation for everlasting victory and glory. His oneness and being called "Messiah" were facts inspired by God, but it was human theologians who gave the Messiah a salvational role and placed his coming at the End-time.

Different Messiahs in Other Jewish Sources

Jewish sources were not unanimous in their depiction of the awaited royal Davidic Messiah who would destroy Israel's enemies and restore its kingdom. He is not always presented as a military leader like his ancestral king.

The Greek *Psalms of Solomon*, which is probably a translation from Hebrew, talks in some detail about the Messiah. This is how one Psalm in this 1st century BCE source describes what the Messiah would do:

> Behold, O Lord, and raise up unto them their king, the son of David, at the time known to you, O God, in order that he may reign over Israel your servant.
>
> And gird him with strength, that he may shatter unrighteous rulers, and that he may purge Jerusalem from gentiles who trample (her) down to destruction.
>
> Wisely, righteously he shall thrust out sinners from (the) inheritance; he shall destroy the arrogance of the sinner as a potter's jar.
>
> With a rod of iron he shall shatter all their substance; he shall destroy the godless nations with the word of his mouth.
>
> At his rebuke nations shall flee before him, and he shall reprove sinners for the thoughts of their heart.
>
> And he shall gather together a holy people, whom he shall lead in righteousness, and he shall judge the tribes of the people who has been made holy by the Lord his God.

But the Messiah will subject all nations and establish the rule of God on earth without resorting to military means, as God will be his source of power:

> For he shall not put his trust in horse and rider and bow, nor shall he multiply for himself gold and silver for war, nor shall he gather confidence from a multitude for the day of battle.

The Lord Himself is his king, the hope of him that is mighty through his hope in God. (PsSol. 17)

While still a military leader, this royal Messiah will not use the normal military means used by his ancestor David, but he will rely on some unclear intervention by God. He is the king, but God is the warrior. David, on the other hand, was a warrior king.

Other interesting intertestamental sources — i.e. belonging to the period between the close of the Old Testament and the beginning of the New Testament — are the *Dead Sea Scrolls*. Mostly written in Hebrew, these manuscripts were discovered in the vicinity of Khirbat Qumran in 1946. Dating from the 2nd century BCE to the 1st century CE, these documents were written by members of a strict, mystical, isolated Jewish sect that is identified with the Essenes. The Jewish Roman historian Flavius Josephus (37-100 CE) is our main source of information about the Essenes. He wrote about them in detail in the *Wars of the Jews* and more briefly in *Antiquities of the Jews*.

As far as the concept of "messiahship" is concerned, the Qumran documents differ significantly from other Jewish sources from the Second Temple era — that is, the period between the reconstruction of the Temple in Jerusalem after the Jews' return from exile to its destruction by the Romans in 70 CE. **First**, the other sources either did not mention the Messiah or gave him only a minor role. **Second**, they did not use the term "Messiah" when talking about that eschatological figure. The Dead Sea Scrolls, on the other hand, give the concept of "messiahship" a lot of prominence and use the term "Messiah."

The Dead Sea Scrolls talk about two awaited Messiahs, one of them descended from David the king, but the other is a descendant of Aaron the priest. It is the priestly Messiah who has the authority. The Davidic Messiah plays no role in the final battle of the Sons of Light against the Sons of Darkness. The priests gather people, but the fighting is done by angels and the final blow is delivered by God himself (Sanders, 1995: 89).

For example, in the following passage, the Old Testament's "branch of David," whom we discussed earlier, is explicitly called "Messiah" (translations are by Wilfred G. E. Watson from *The Dead Sea Scrolls*):

A sovereign shall [not] be removed from the tribe of Judah. While Israel has the dominion, there will [not] lack someone who sits on the throne of David. For "the staff" is the covenant of royalty, [and the thou]sands of Israel are "the feet." [*Blank*] Until the messiah of justice comes, the branch of David. For to him and to his descendants (to them) has been given the covenant of royalty over his people for all everlasting generations, which he has observed. (4Q252:1–5)

The royal Messiah, like King David, is a warrior. The Messiah will destroy his enemies and rule over all people, according to another scroll:

> [The interpretation of the word concerns the shoot] of David which will sprout [in the final days, since] [with the breath of his lips he will execute] his enemies and God will support him with [the spirit of] courage [. . .] [. . .] throne of glory, [holy] crown and hemmed vestments [. . .] in his hand. He will rule over all the peoples and Magog [. . .] his sword will judge all the peoples. And as for what he says: "He will not [judge by appearances] or give verdicts on hearsay," its interpretation: [. . .] according to what they teach him, he will judge, and upon his mouth [. . .] with him will go out one of the priests of renown, holding clothes in his hand. (4Q161:18-25)

This passage does not use the term "Messiah" but it clearly talks about him.

Like the *Psalms of Solomon*, the Dead Sea Scrolls make the king-Messiah subordinate to a second Messiah who is a priest:

> They should not depart from any counsel of the law in order to walk in complete stubbornness of their heart, but instead shall be ruled by the first directives which the men of the Community began to be taught until the prophet comes, and the Messiahs of Aaron and Israel. (1QS IX 9–11)

The "Messiah of Israel" is the royal savior and the "Messiah of Aaron" is the priestly one, as Aaron was a priest in the Old Testament. There are a number of such texts that talk about two Messiahs.

The Dead Sea Scrolls seem to talk about yet more eschatological figures. There is one referred to as the "prophet," in the passage above. Scholars have identified yet another messianic figure who, unlike the others, seems to be heavenly. Such a figure is also seen in two other works which might have been influenced by Christians: 1 Enoch 37-71 and 4 Ezra 13. For a detailed investigation of the concept of "messiahship" in the Dead Sea scrolls the reader may consult *Messianic Hopes in the Qumran Writings* in *The People of the Dead Sea Scrolls* (Martinez & Barrera, 1995).

Among the different Messiahs that may be identified one way or another in the scripture, the one described as the "son of David" is the most prominent:

> This diversity of messianic figures and their function should not obscure the prime importance of the Davidic messiah. Messianic expectation was not universal; both those who chose to speculate in this vein had, in the classical prophetic texts and later apocalyptic interpretations of them, a readily available body of tradition to draw on. The Messiah son of David is the best and most widely attested figure, cutting across sectarian as well as temporal lines. We can trace him from the classical Jewish biblical histories and prophets through the multitudinous intertestamental texts just reviewed on into rabbinic prayers and benedictions. His role in

history's final drama was clear. "See, Lord, and raise up for them their king, the son of David," prayed the author of the pseudonymous Psalms of Solomon some time in the first century BCE, "at the time that you have knowledge of [i.e., the Endtime], and gird him with strength, so he may smash those who rule without justice" (17:23). Executing Judgment, defeating the enemies of God, reigning over a restored Israel, establishing unending peace, this eschatological prince epitomized the military prowess, valor, and virtues of his royal ancestor, the warrior king David. (Fredriksen, 2001: 124)

Clearly, the prominence of the military Davidic Messiah originates from his embodiment of the hope for the restoration of Israel. However, the belief that God will send the Messiah, who is a descendant of David, at the end times to effect Israel's redemption was not adopted by all Jews (Fredriksen, 2001: 129).

To recap on what we discussed in this chapter, the term "Messiah" is used in the Old Testament for various historical figures but never for a future one. On the other hand, the Jewish scripture contains prophecies about a number of future salvational figures, although none is called "Messiah." Such passages became seen as carrying messianic expectations after the figures they talk about where linked to the concept of "the Messiah." This concept was inspired by a revelation from God, but it was changed as a result of Israel's troubled history and its perceived need for a military savior to restore its independent kingdom. Some Jewish groups also believed in the coming of more than one Messiah.

2

The Christ in the New Testament

The term "Messiah" appears in the Greek New Testament as many as 571 times — 569 as *Christos* (Χριστός), from which "Christ" is derived, and twice as *Messias* (Μεσσίας) (John 1:41, 4:25). Mark, the oldest of the four Gospels, has the term Christ only 7 times, whereas Matthew uses it 16 times, Luke 11, and John 20. All New Testament writers recognize Jesus as the Christ.

The significantly higher number and frequency with which the term appears in the New Testament as opposed to the Old Testament reflect the substantially bigger role of the concept of the Messiah in Christianity. In contrast to its minor role in the Old Testament, this concept takes centre stage in the New Testament. Jewish intertestamental writings showed more interest in the Messiah than the Old Testament writers did, as the Messiah was becoming a more central figure in Jewish salvational theology. But that interest came nowhere near the status that Christian authors and, accordingly, their audiences gave to the Messiah in the new religion. One manifestation of this interest is the large number of Old Testament *prophecies* that the Gospel writers used to show that Jesus was the awaited Messiah.

Unanointed Messiah

Significantly, Jesus was not properly anointed, as the Jewish authorities and most Jews did not accept his messiahship. The Gospels report an event in which Jesus was anointed by a woman:

> And while he was at Bethany in the house of Simon the leper, as he was reclining at table, a woman came with an alabaster flask of ointment of pure nard, very costly, and she broke the flask and poured it over his head. There were some who said to themselves indignantly, "Why was the ointment wasted like that? For this ointment could have been sold for more than three hundred denarii and given to the poor." And they scolded her. But Jesus said, "Leave her alone. Why do you trouble her? She has done a beautiful thing to me. For you always have the poor with you, and whenever you want, you can do good for them. But you will not always have me. She has done what she could; she has anointed my body beforehand for burial. And truly, I say to you, wherever the gospel is

proclaimed in the whole world, what she has done will be told in memory of her." (Mark 14:3-9)

This incident is also mentioned by Matthew (26:6-13) and, with significant differences, by John (12:1-8). Luke (7:36-50) has an account that shares similarities with the other three Gospels, but it has also significant differences. It is probably a different version of the same event — a common phenomenon in the Gospels.

This casual anointment by a laywoman cannot be seen as the equivalent of anointing Jesus as the Messiah. Anointment was performed by a priest or prophet. Far from being anointed as the Messiah, Jesus was shunned by the Jewish religious authorities who considered him a heretic.

Furthermore, anointment, according to the Old Testament, was done using a specially prepared holy oil, which is described in God's following words to Moses:

> Take the finest spices: of liquid myrrh 500 shekels, and of sweet-smelling cinnamon half as much, that is, 250, and 250 of aromatic cane, and 500 of cassia, according to the shekel of the sanctuary, and a hin of olive oil. And you shall make these a sacred anointing oil blended as by the perfumer; it shall be a holy anointing oil. (Exo. 30:23-25)

Finally, the anointment event above took place late in Jesus' ministry when he was already being seen as the awaited Messiah. So the implication of the Gospels is that Jesus' messiahship was not declared or endorsed by an official religious ceremony of anointment.

The Christ of Paul

Paul's letters are the earliest books of the New Testament and where the term "Christ" makes most of its appearances. Paul uses the term "Christ" as a proper name not title, hence the very common phrase "Jesus Christ" in his writings. He does not explicitly explain his understanding of Christhood. His use of the term Christ seems to suggest that he presumed people understood what Christ meant. Because of this silence, it is difficult to be certain what Paul understood Christ to mean.

Paul's Jesus is a spiritual figure who came to redeem people, by being crucified and raised from the dead. It is possible that this is what Paul took the term Christ to mean. It is not clear where he would have got this unique understanding from. It is not derived from his Jewish background, nor is it an image that we find in the Gospels to suggest that it was already shared by other early Christians.

Additionally, Paul shows almost complete lack of interest in the historical Jesus, which is partly due to his ignorance of that history:

> Apart from the crucifixion and resurrection, the only other event in Jesus' life mentioned by Paul is Jesus' Last Supper with his disciples (1 Cor. 11:23-27)! He does not talk about Jesus' birth, miracles, encounters with the Jewish leaders, arrest, or trial. Even his crucifixion and resurrection are cited mainly in the context of talking about their spiritual and theological significance; their historical details are never mentioned. Not even the headlines of the when, where, and how of these most important events are recorded. (Fatoohi, 2008: 93)

Over the centuries, most Christians shared Paul's disinterest in the historical Jesus and almost complete concentration on the crucified and risen Jesus. The crucifixion and resurrection became the central events in Jesus' life and all of his history is understood in the light of its relation to these events. Despite his clear detachment from Jesus' life, Paul succeeded in developing the dominant theology in Christianity, which he built on the crucifixion and resurrection of Jesus.

Paul's ignorance and neglect of the historical Jesus is why our main sources of information about the Christ in the New Testament have to be the four Gospels. The Evangelists were much more interested in Jesus' history. It is also probably safe to presume that the Gospel writers knew more about the historical Jesus than Paul did.

However, the Evangelists gave us four different and, at times, contradictory accounts. Each account also contains inconsistencies. We should embrace ourselves for some hard work with passages that are not always in harmony and are, at times, outright contradictory.

3

Al-Masīh in the Qur'an

Jesus is called *al-Masīh* (the Messiah) 11 times in 9 different verses in the Qur'an. It occurs 3 times alone (4.172, 5.72, 9.30), 3 times in the phrase "the Messiah, Jesus son of Mary" (3.45, 4.157, 4.171), and 5 times in "the Messiah son of Mary" (5.17, 5.72, 5.75, 9.31). All 9 verses are quoted in Appendix A for reference.

The Meaning of *Masīh*

The Qur'an does not explain the meaning of the term *al-Masīh*. The prefix *al* is the Arabic definite article, indicating that *al-Masīh* is not a name but a title. Muslim exegetes have different opinions about the etymology and meaning of the word *Masīh*. In his commentary on verse 2.40, al-Qurṭubī mentions the view of some that the term is a name which is not derived from another word. Later in his comments on verse 3.45, he cites the opinion that *Masīh* means "truthful," but he also gives several different views on the origin of this term, relating it to the root *mash* and its different meanings in different contexts:

- **Wander**: he was a wanderer who never settled in one place.
- **Rub**: whenever he rubbed a disable person the disability was cured.
- **Anoint**: he was anointed with the good smelling oil of blessedness with which prophets were anointed. This refers to Jesus' saying about himself: "He has made me blessed wherever I may be" (19.31).
- **Flat**: he had flat feet.
- **Cleanse**: he was cleansed of sins and was purified.
- **Give someone good looks**: he was given good looks.

This list still does not include all meanings that scholars have associated with the word *Masīh*. Aṭ-Ṭabāṭabā'ī, for instance, who mentions some of the meanings above, gives other meanings that link the word to the verb *masaha* or "rub": Gabriel "rubbed" Jesus at his birth with his wings to protect him from Satan; Jesus used to "rub" on the heads of orphans; and Jesus used to "rub" on the eyes of the blind to make them see. As-Sha'rāwī (1999: 9-14) cites 23 meanings of *Masīḥ* that al-Qurṭubī attributes to various exegetes, as well as other meanings suggested by other scholars.

The title "Messiah" does not look like being used in verses that talk about specific issues, so it does not seem possible to study the Qur'anic meaning of "Messiah" by analyzing its contexts.

Messiahship is No Special Prophethood

Jesus is described in the Qur'an as one of the most favored prophets, but the fact that he was the Messiah is not presented as the reason for this special status or as a differentiator. God says in the Qur'an that He gave some prophets higher statuses than others, with one verse citing the revelation of a divine book to David as one differentiating favor:

> Your Lord [O Muhammad!] best knows who is in the heavens and the earth. We conferred on some prophets more favor than others, and to David did we give a book. (17.55)

In another verse, the Qur'an repeats the fact that God elevated some prophets over others and mentions Jesus as one of those specially favored, identifying two special divine favors:

> Those are the messengers. We conferred on some more favor than on others. Among them there are some to whom Allah spoke, while some of them He exalted [above others] in degree; and We gave Jesus son of Mary clear proofs and We supported him with the Spirit of Holiness (Gabriel). (from 2.253)

The two special favors to Jesus were giving him "clear proofs," meaning miracles, and supporting him with Gabriel, who was involved in the miracle of the virginal conception. These favors were not unique to Jesus. Other prophets, such as Moses, performed miracles, and others, such as Muhammad, were contacted by Gabriel. Messiahship, while unique, is not cited as one of those special favors. Equally significant is the fact that in this verse Jesus is referred to with his name and the title "son of Mary," which is another reference to the fact that he was miraculously conceived, but not with his title of the Messiah. So, Jesus' messiahship is not presented in the Qur'an as a differentiator or as an explanation of his status as one of the most favored prophets.

The Awaited Messiah

One verse states that when the angels brought to Mary the news about the miracle of her virginal conception, they told her that her miraculous son would be known as "the Messiah," "Jesus," and "son of Mary":

> When the angels said: "O Mary! Allah gives you the good news of a Word from Him, whose name is the Messiah, Jesus son of Mary, who is illustrious in this world and the hereafter, and who is one of those brought near [to Allah]. (3.45)

The verse suggests that the title of *the Messiah* was already familiar to Mary. This is in line with the established fact that at the time of Jesus' birth the concept of *the Messiah* was well known. The verse also supports my view that *the Messiah* was a concept that God had revealed. The Qur'an could not be confirming a concept that was developed by the Jews or later the Christians, but it is stressing the divine origin of the prophecy about the coming of *the Messiah*. This prophecy is not cited in the Qur'an, as mentioning it over 6 centuries after it was fulfilled and at the time of a new Prophet, Muhammad, would not have served any purpose.

While Mary, like other Jews, knew of the coming of the Messiah, it was only when she received the news from Gabriel about the birth of Jesus that she knew that she was chosen to be the mother of *the Messiah*.

One Messiah

The use of the definite article in *al-Masīḥ* may suggest that the Qur'an implies that there was only one Messiah. Indeed, nowhere does the Qur'an mention any other Messiah, whether past or future. Even though the term "Messiah" was used in the Old Testament for different individuals, the Qur'an mentions only one Messiah: Jesus. This *may* but *does not necessarily* mean that the Qur'an implies that there was only one Messiah. If it does, this would still not mean that the Qur'an denies the historicity of those anointed figures in the Old Testament, but it would probably imply that the term "Messiah" was mistakenly applied to those historical men in the Old Testament. Note how, for instance, King David was a Messiah in the Old Testament, but the Qur'an does not call him so, even though it considers David a prophet, which is a very special status shared with men like Jesus, Moses, and Muhammad.

The Qur'an, then, supports the Christian sources in speaking about one Messiah only. It also agrees with them in identifying this Messiah with Jesus.

On the other hand, in the only three verses where it is mentioned alone, the title *Masīḥ* is identified with Jesus either by name or by calling him "son of Mary" in the same verse or in an adjacent one. This may be seen as identifying Jesus from other Messiahs:

> O People of the Book! Commit no excesses in your religion or utter anything concerning Allah but the truth. The Messiah, Jesus son of Mary, was only a messenger of Allah, His Word that He sent to Mary, and a Spirit from Him [that He sent]. So believe in Allah and His messengers, and do not say "Three." Desist, it is better for you! Allah is one God. Far exalted is He above having offspring. His is all that is in the heavens and all that is on the earth. Allah is sufficient a disposer of affairs. (4.171) The Messiah would never scorn to be a servant to Allah, nor would the angels who are nearest to Allah. As for those who scorn His service and are arrogantly proud, He shall gather them all to Himself to answer. (4.172)

> Surely they disbelieve those who say: "Allah is the Messiah son of Mary." The Messiah himself said: "O Children of Israel! Worship Allah, my Lord and your Lord. Whoever joins other gods with Allah, for him Allah has forbidden paradise. His abode is the Fire. The evildoers shall have no helpers." (5.72)

> The Jews say: "'Uzayr is the son of Allah", and the Christians say: "The Messiah is the son of Allah". That is a saying from their mouths, imitating the saying of the disbelievers of old. May Allah fight them! How deluded they are! (9.30) They have taken their rabbis and monks as lords besides Allah, and so they treated the Messiah son of Mary, although they were not commanded to worship other than One God; there is no God save Him. Far exalted is He above their attribution of partners to Him! (9.31)

However, as the Qur'an *explicitly* mentions only one Messiah, any suggestion to the contrary would be completely speculative, even if it cannot be totally dismissed.

The Name of the Followers of the Messiah

The Qur'an does not use the title "Christ" to call Jesus' followers "Christians." Christians are not named after the title "Messiah" but are called *Naṣārā* or "Nazarenes." This Qur'anic title does not presume that Jesus was a Nazarene. It is derived from a particular historical event in which Jesus called on his companions for "support" or *naṣr* in Arabic (also 61.14) (Fatoohi, 2007: 224-229):

> But when Jesus perceived disbelief on their part, he said: "Who are my *anṣār* (supporters) in the cause of Allah?" The companions said: "We are Allah's *anṣār*. We believe in Allah, and do you bear witness that we are Muslims." (3.52)

Like the Qur'an, and contrary to what many think, the term *Christianos* (Χριστιανός) or "Christian" is never used in the Gospels. Furthermore, it appears only three times in the New Testament — twice in Acts and once in the First Epistle of Peter. The first mention in Acts is particularly significant: "For a whole year they met with the church and taught a great many people. And in Antioch the disciples were first called Christians" (Acts 11:26). This visit of the apostles Paul and Barnabas to Antioch occurred around 45 CE. This suggests that it was well after Jesus had gone that *his disciples* or any of his followers started to be known as "Christians."

The term is then used twice to refer to *any follower of the Christ*, which is what it ultimately came to mean. In its second occurrence in Acts (26:28), King Agrippa II argues with Paul for trying to convert him to a "Christian." In the third and last appearance of the term in the New Testament, the follower of the Christ is reminded not to be ashamed of suffering as a "Christian" and to glorify God for bearing such a name (1 Peter 4:16).

It may be suggested that it was Paul and Barnabas who introduced this term in Antioch. One argument against this view is that Paul never uses the term in his letters, preferring to call fellow Christians *adelphos* (brothers) and *adelphen* (sisters). This may indicate that the term was introduced by non-Christians, which could explain Acts' anonymous attribution of the coining of the term. If that is the case, it is doubtful that the term was first applied to Christ's disciples and then to all his followers, as non-Christians would not have differentiated between the two.

In the following chapters, we will discuss the different identities and attributes that the Evangelists presented the Christ through and examine each one of them from the Qur'an's perspective. Where relevant, we will also make references to Jewish writings about the Messiah.

4

Jesus' Public Claim to Messiahship

Some New Testament scholars have questioned whether Jesus thought of himself as a Messiah (Sanders, 1995: 241-242). Some of those who accepted he did still cast doubt over whether he ever called himself so (Parrinder, 1995: 32). It is true that there is no Gospel passage in which Jesus uses the term "Christ" to refer to himself or goes out of his way to ask people to call him so, but there is clear evidence in the Gospels to refute both views above. There are a number of statements attributed to Jesus that leave no doubt that he claimed to be the Messiah, even if these were in response to a question or statement from someone else.

Mark and Luke (9:20-21) recount that when Jesus asked his disciples whom they thought he was, Peter replied that Jesus was the Christ. Jesus responded by commanding the disciples not to tell anyone:

> And Jesus went on with his disciples to the villages of Caesarea Philippi. And on the way he asked his disciples, "Who do people say that I am?" And they told him, "John the Baptist; and others say, Elijah; and others, one of the prophets." And he asked them, "But who do you say that I am?" Peter answered him, "You are the Christ." And he strictly charged them to tell no one about him. (Mark 8:27-30)

This *implies* that Jesus confirmed that he was the Christ but did not want that to be made public for some reason.

Matthew (16:17-20) also reports this story, but he changes Jesus' reply to one that is more *explicitly* endorsing of Peter's words: "Blessed are you, Simon Bar-Jonah! For flesh and blood has not revealed this to you, but my Father who is in heaven." He then reiterates Mark's and Luke's statements that Jesus "strictly charged the disciples to tell no one that he was the Christ."

Luke recounts another incident in which Jesus did not allow demons to reveal that he was the Christ:

> Now when the sun was setting, all those who had any who were sick with various diseases brought them to him, and he laid his hands on every one of them and healed them. And demons also came out of many, crying, "You are the Son of God!" But he rebuked them and would not allow them to speak, because they knew that he was the Christ. (Luke 4:40-41)

John reports an encounter between Jesus and a Samaritan woman in which he clearly tells the woman that he was the awaited Messiah:

> The woman said to him, "I know that Messiah is coming (he who is called Christ). When he comes, he will tell us all things." Jesus said to her, "I who speak to you am he." Just then his disciples came back. They marveled that he was talking with a woman, but no one said, "What do you seek?" or, "Why are you talking with her?" So the woman left her water jar and went away into town and said to the people, "Come, see a man who told me all that I ever did. Can this be the Christ?" They went out of the town and were coming to him. (John 4:25-30)

The fact that Jesus was being publicly called the Christ is also confirmed when Pilate, discussing with the Jewish leader what to do with Jesus after he had questioned him, describes him as the one "who is called Christ" (Matt. 27:17, 27:22).

Reports of Jesus' trial contain his most explicit claim to being the Christ. When asked by the high priest if he was the Christ, Jesus told him "you have said so," according to Matthew (26:64). Jesus' reply according to Mark (14:62) is even more emphatic: "I am."

Luke has a slightly different story:

> When day came, the assembly of the elders of the people gathered together, both chief priests and scribes. And they led him away to their council, and they said, "If you are the Christ, tell us." But he said to them, "If I tell you, you will not believe, and if I ask you, you will not answer." (Luke 22:66-68)

Jesus' words must imply that his answer would have been "yes," and that if the priests and scribes were honest, then they would also have answered that question with a yes. Luke (23:2) also later states that the Jewish elders accused Jesus of claiming to be the Christ.

John cites an incident before the trial which suggests that Jesus had already told his Jewish audience that he is the Christ and that they did not believe him:

> So the Jews gathered around him and said to him, "How long will you keep us in suspense? If you are the Christ, tell us plainly." Jesus answered them, "I told you, and you do not believe. The works that I do in my Father's name bear witness about me." (John 10:24-25)

Another confirmation that Jesus declared himself as the Christ may also be read in Jesus' following warning to his disciples on the Mount of Olives (also Matt. 24:23-24):

> And then if anyone says to you, "Look, here is the Christ!" or "Look, there he is!" do not believe it. For false christs and false prophets will

arise and perform signs and wonders, to lead astray, if possible, the elect. (Mark 13:21-22)

Jesus' warning implies that he was the *true Christ*.
Mark reports this earlier warning on the Mount of Olives:

And Jesus began to say to them, "See that no one leads you astray. Many will come in my name, saying, 'I am he!' and they will lead many astray. (Mark 13:5-6)

This warning, which is also found in Matthew (24:4-5), suggests that there was no shortage of claimants to the role of the Messiah, but it also means that Jesus considered and declared himself as "the Christ."

The emphasis that Jesus is the only Christ may also be seen in his words to people and his disciples: "Neither be called instructors, for you have one instructor, the Christ" (Matt. 23:10).

The Evangelists also attribute to Jesus a number of sayings in which he interprets scriptural passages as referring to him. Two of these texts about future saviors do not use the term "Messiah," but the implication of the Gospels is that Jesus understood the passages to be Messianic and taught that he was the awaited Messiah (also John 13:18-21):

And the scroll of the prophet Isaiah was given to him. He unrolled the scroll and found the place where it was written, "The Spirit of the Lord is upon me, because he has anointed me to proclaim good news to the poor. He has sent me to proclaim liberty to the captives and recovering of sight to the blind, to set at liberty those who are oppressed, to proclaim the year of the Lord's favor." And he rolled up the scroll and gave it back to the attendant and sat down. And the eyes of all in the synagogue were fixed on him. And he began to say to them, "Today this Scripture has been fulfilled in your hearing." (Luke 4:17-21)

You search the Scriptures because you think that in them you have eternal life; and it is they that bear witness about me. (John 5:39)

On the last day of the feast, the great day, Jesus stood up and cried out, "If anyone thirsts, let him come to me and drink. Whoever believes in me, as the Scripture has said, 'Out of his heart will flow rivers of living water.'" (John 7:37-38)

Luke also mentions two instances in which Jesus cites alleged scriptural prophecies about the suffering of the Christ which he applies to himself, making it clear that he meant that he was the Messiah:

And he said to them, "O foolish ones, and slow of heart to believe all that the prophets have spoken! Was it not necessary that the Christ should suffer these things and enter into his glory?" (Luke 24:25-26)

Then he said to them, "These are my words that I spoke to you while I was still with you, that everything written about me in the Law of Moses and the Prophets and the Psalms must be fulfilled." Then he opened their minds to understand the Scriptures, and said to them, "Thus it is written, that the Christ should suffer and on the third day rise from the dead." (Luke 24:44-46)

However, there are no such prophecies in the Old Testament! In fact, the concept of the suffering Messiah is itself a Christian invention, as we shall discuss in detail in Chapter 10. So these sayings are no evidence that Jesus said that he was the Messiah, because he could not have cited passages and a concept that were invented only after him. But these anachronistic passages show that the Evangelists believed that he publicly proclaimed his messiahship.

In my view, the Gospels leave no room for questioning the fact that Jesus believed that he was the Christ and that he let people know that. Admittedly, the Gospel authors are rather contradictory as to whether he wanted his claim to messiahship to be made completely public or not.

If Jesus' reported attempts to limit the use of the title "Christ" were true, they must reflect his efforts to detach himself from the political and nationalistic expectations that people had attached to this title.

Theissen and Merz (1999: 553) make an important point as to why Jesus must have been called the Christ in his life rather than after his supposed crucifixion and resurrection. Noting that the crucifixion and the rising from death became seen as the most important events in Jesus' life, these scholars go on to note:

> The title Messiah would have been unsuitable for interpreting a life which focussed on the cross and resurrection. There is no evidence prior to the New Testament for the notion of a suffering Messiah; moreover, there is no evidence of anyone becoming the Messiah through resurrection. Therefore the title Messiah must already have been associated with Jesus if it was to live on after Easter: it could not have interpreted the cross and resurrection, but the cross and resurrection could have given it a deeper meaning. (Theissen & Merz, 1999: 540)

Jesus must have been called the Christ in his life. Also, it is difficult to see how this title could have spread without at least his implicit consent.

The Qur'anic Jesus' public Proclamation of Messiahship

In the Qur'an, Jesus is called the Messiah by God (4.171, 4.172, 5.17, 5.72, 5.75, 9.31), angels (3.45), and his followers (5.17, 5.72, 9.30). Those who rejected him, including the Jews, also called him the Messiah (4.157), but that is to identify him rather than to accept his messiahship. Jesus is not cited in the Qur'an as calling himself the Messiah, but that is because there are only a few statements attributed to him, and even fewer in which he talks about himself.

Jesus told people that he was a prophet who was given wisdom, a divine book called the Injīl, and knowledge of the Torah, and that he had the authority to perform miracles, which he proved by performing a number of impressive miracles:

> He said: "I am Allah's servant. He has given me the Book and has appointed me a prophet." (19.30)
>
> And when Jesus son of Mary said: "O Children of Israel! I am a messenger of Allah to you, confirming that which was revealed before me of the Torah, and bringing good news about a messenger who will come after me, whose name is Aḥmad." But when he came to them with clear proofs, they said: "This is clear magic." (61.6)
>
> And [He shall make him] a messenger to the Children of Israel, saying: "I have come to you with a sign from your Lord. I create for you out of clay the figures of birds, then I breathe into it [the clay], and it becomes birds by Allah's permission. I heal the blind person and the albino; I raise the dead, by Allah's permission. And I tell you what you eat and what you store in your houses. Herein verily is a sign for you, if you are to be believers." (3.49)

Jesus could not have told people all of this but concealed the fact that he was the Messiah. He must have announced publicly his messiahship. In fact, we have to accept that people realized that Jesus was the Messiah because he told them so — a claim that was confirmed by his miracles.

Nevertheless, it is not unreasonable to suggest that at times, probably near the end of his mission, he had to be rather reticent about the title Messiah because of its *Jewish* political connotations. Jesus was not the military leader that the Jews thought the awaited Messiah would be, and he would not have wanted the Jewish misguided image of the Messiah to cause him problems with the Roman authorities.

5

King of the Jews?

The Gospels confirm that the Jews were waiting for the coming of the Messiah who would liberate Israel and restore its kingdom. One piece of evidence from the Gospels comes from Luke who has the following to say about a man who lived at the time of Jesus' birth:

> Now there was a man in Jerusalem, whose name was Simeon, and this man was righteous and devout, waiting for the consolation of Israel, and the Holy Spirit was upon him. And it had been revealed to him by the Holy Spirit that he would not see death before he had seen the Lord's Christ. (Luke 2:25-26)

When Simeon met baby Jesus in the temple, he took him in his arms and started praying:

> Lord, now you are letting your servant depart in peace, according to your word; for my eyes have seen your salvation that you have prepared in the presence of all peoples, a light for revelation to the Gentiles, and for glory to your people Israel. (Luke 2:29-32)

Then a prophetess called Anna also spoke about Jesus to "all who were waiting for the redemption of Jerusalem" (Luke 2:38).

Given the Messiah's role in the restoration of Israel, it is natural that he was associated with the kingship of the Jews. The Messiah would bring good to the Gentiles also, according to Simeon.

Jesus the King Messiah

We have already seen in the Old Testament that kings, in addition to priests and prophets, were anointed, and that the awaited Messiah is seen by the Jews as a king. This view has resulted in Jesus also being seen in this way by those who accepted his messiahship.

Matthew's account of Jesus' story of birth shows that Herod took the title "king of the Jews" to mean "the Christ." Not only Herod, but people in general are shown to have understood "the Christ" in this sense. In fact, "king of the Jews" is the most emphasized meaning of "the Christ" in the Gospels. The term "king of the Jews" is not always explicitly associated with the title "the Christ," but the context makes it clear that Jesus was called king because he was considered to be the Christ. Let's review some of the passages that describe Jesus as a king.

Luke (19:38) tells us that Jesus' disciples praised him as "the King who comes in the name of the Lord." Stunned by what Jesus knew about him, a Nathanael called Jesus "the king of Israel" (John 1:49).

Mark, Mathew, and Luke — who are known as the "Synoptics" because of their similarities to each other — depict Jesus' last entry into Jerusalem very much like that of a king (also Matt. 21:7-9; Luke 19:35-38):

> And they brought the colt to Jesus and threw their cloaks on it, and he sat on it. And many spread their cloaks on the road, and others spread leafy branches that they had cut from the fields. And those who went before and those who followed were shouting, "Hosanna! Blessed is he who comes in the name of the Lord! Blessed is the coming kingdom of our father David! Hosanna in the highest!" And he entered Jerusalem and went into the temple. (Mark 11:7-11)

John's version (12:12-15) of this story is quite different, but he still shares with the Synoptists one particularly interesting detail in the proclamation of the crowd. The shouting of the crowd according to Mark is quoted above; Matthew has them praise: "Hosanna to the Son of David! Blessed is he who comes in the name of the Lord! Hosanna in the highest!"; Luke has them shout: "Blessed is the King who comes in the name of the Lord! Peace in heaven and glory in the highest!"; and accordingly to John, they said: "Hosanna! Blessed is he who comes in the name of the Lord, even the King of Israel!" Mark, Luke, and John clearly make the crowd recognize Jesus as the king of Israel. Matthew does that in a more implicit way by having them call Jesus the "Son of David." Matthew also differs from the other three Evangelists by presenting Jesus' entry as the fulfillment of a scriptural prophecy about the Messiah.

Explaining to Pilate Jesus' charges, the Jewish leaders said: "We found this man misleading our nation and forbidding us to give tribute to Caesar, and saying that he himself is Christ, a king" (Luke 23:2). When they found that Pilate started to sympathize with Jesus and think of releasing him, they used Jesus' supposed claim to kingship, which is what they understood messiahship to mean, to suggest that Jesus was challenging Caesar and that Pilate would not be acting as Caesar's ally if he tolerated that:

> From then on Pilate sought to release him, but the Jews cried out, "If you release this man, you are not Caesar's friend. Everyone who makes himself a king opposes Caesar." So when Pilate heard these words, he brought Jesus out and sat down on the judgment seat at a place called The Stone Pavement, and in Aramaic Gabbatha. Now it was the day of Preparation of the Passover. It was about the sixth hour. He said to the

Jews, "Behold your King!" They cried out, "Away with him, away with him, crucify him!" Pilate said to them, "Shall I crucify your King?" The chief priests answered, "We have no king but Caesar." (John 19:12-15)

The Jewish leaders also mocked Jesus on the cross saying: "Let the Christ, the King of Israel, come down now from the cross that we may see and believe" (Mark 15:32). The four Evangelists report that during his crucifixion, Jesus was sarcastically referred to as "king of the Jews" (e.g. Mark 15:18; Matt. 27:29; Luke 23:37; John 19:3). The titulus over the cross also called Jesus "king of the Jews" (Mark 15:26; Matt. 27:37; Luke 23:38; John 19:19).

Jesus the Spiritual King Messiah

The accusation that Jesus sought to become king of the Jews is first met in the Gospels during Jesus' trial. But the accounts of this trial are full of historical inaccuracies in addition to internal inconsistencies (Fatoohi, 2008). Furthermore, this accusation is presented as false. The Synoptics agree that when Pilate asked Jesus whether he claimed to be the king of the Jews Jesus answered: "You have said so" (Mark 15:2; Matt. 27:11; Luke 23:3). John gives a different, more detailed answer in which Jesus makes the extremely significant declaration that his kingdom was not of this world:

> So Pilate entered his headquarters again and called Jesus and said to him, "Are you the King of the Jews?" Jesus answered, "Do you say this of your own accord, or did others say it to you about me?" Pilate answered, "Am I a Jew? Your own nation and the chief priests have delivered you over to me. What have you done?" Jesus answered, "My kingdom is not of this world. If my kingdom were of this world, my servants would have been fighting, that I might not be delivered over to the Jews. But my kingdom is not from the world." Then Pilate said to him, "So you are a king?" Jesus answered, "You say that I am a king. For this purpose I was born and for this purpose I have come into the world — to bear witness to the truth. Everyone who is of the truth listens to my voice." Pilate said to him, "What is truth?" After he had said this, he went back outside to the Jews and told them, "I find no guilt in him." (John 18:33-38)

Jesus told Pilate that kings on earth are appointed by people, but his appointment came from God, so his kingdom was not earthly. His kingdom was heavenly, not the kind of earthly kingdom that the Jews were expecting the Messiah to establish.

The four Gospels use the expression "kingdom of God" over 50 times and Matthew uses also the equivalent term "kingdom of heaven" over 30 times. These expressions occur mainly in sayings attributed to Jesus. It is a kingdom that can be entered only by those who "turn around and become like little children" (Matt. 18:3; also Mark 10:15 and Luke 18:17). It is clearly a spiritual kingdom. This is how Pilate also understood Jesus and thus concluded that there was no basis for the charges against him. This is probably also why the author of the Gospel of Mark makes Pilate, speaking to the Jews, refer to Jesus as the "one you call king of the Jews" (Mark 15:12).

John reports another interesting incident in which Jesus refused to be portrayed as king and avoided any attempt to drag him into politics. It happened after Jesus' miracle of feeding five thousand people:

> When the people saw the sign that he had done, they said, "This is indeed the Prophet who is to come into the world!" Perceiving then that they were about to come and take him by force to make him king, Jesus withdrew again to the mountain by himself. (John 6:14-15)

Jesus' teaching that the Christ was not an earthly king might also be read from his insistence that the Christ could not have been a "son of David" (Mark 12:35-37; Matt. 22:41-46; Luke 20:41-44). While the Synoptists call him the "son of David," in the only time that Jesus himself is quoted about this issue, he denies it!

John severs another alleged link between Jesus and King David. Both Matthew and Luke claim that Jesus was born in Bethlehem, in order to link him to David. John's Jesus is a Galilean who has no link with Bethlehem:

> Others said, "This is the Christ." But some said, "Is the Christ to come from Galilee? Has not the Scripture said that the Christ comes from the offspring of David, and comes from Bethlehem, the village where David was?" So there was a division among the people over him. (John 7:41-43)

Mark also has no reference to Jesus being linked to Bethlehem. Mark and John (p. 56) make Nazareth Jesus' place of birth.

The Gospels contain reports of Jesus trying at times to keep his identity as the Christ secret (Mark 8:29-30; Matt. 16:20; Luke 4:41, 9:20-21). If authentic, these reports reflect his attempts to reject anything linking him to the kingship of the Jews, not hide his identity as the Christ.

Jesus the Messiah as a Spiritual Leader

Not only refusing to be portrayed as king, Jesus also avoided giving any indication that he may represent any political threat to the rulers (also Matt. 22:16-21; Luke 20:22-25):

> And they came and said to him, "Teacher, we know that you are true and do not care about anyone's opinion. For you are not swayed by appearances, but truly teach the way of God. Is it lawful to pay taxes to Caesar, or not? Should we pay them, or should we not?" But, knowing their hypocrisy, he said to them, "Why put me to the test? Bring me a denarius and let me look at it." And they brought one. And he said to them, "Whose likeness and inscription is this?" They said to him, "Caesar's." Jesus said to them, "Render to Caesar the things that are Caesar's, and to God the things that are God's." And they marveled at him. (Mark 12:14-17)

I fully agree with professor Geza Vermes (2000: 181) that "contrary to the claim of some contemporary New Testament interpreters, the general context of the portrait of Jesus in the Synoptics and in the rest of the New Testament shows that he was not a pretender to the throne of David, or a would-be leader of a revolt against Rome." Even though Luke (1:32) claims that Gabriel told Mary about Jesus that "the Lord God will give him the throne of his father David," Jesus was not only never given that throne, but he also never sought it.

Nothing in what the Gospels recorded of Jesus' sayings or works indicates in any way that he tried to establish or even thought of founding an earthly kingdom or had any political ambitions. The few Roman sources from the 1st and 2nd centuries CE that mention Jesus are equally void of any suggestions that he laid claim to the kingship of the Jews. Jewish sources also do not provide any evidence that Jesus claimed to be the king of Jews. The Christian concept of Jesus being a king is clearly inherited from the Jewish tradition where the Messiah is seen as an earthly military king who would liberate the Israelites and reestablish their lost kingdom. The fact that, according to the Gospels, the Jews had to alert Pilate to Jesus' danger is in line with the fact that Jesus did not do anything to draw the attention of the Roman authorities. Pilate entered the story of Jesus only after the Jews contacted him.

Jesus confirmed that he was the Christ, but he also disapproved of what the concept of the Christ had become. For him, the Christ was a spiritual prophet and teacher, not someone with a political or secular agenda. The Messiah was a reformer who would lay down again the foundations of the religion of Abraham, Jacob, Moses, Aaron, and all other Israelite prophets. This rather unpopular image of the Messiah is probably why only a small minority of the Jews, not many thousands as suggested by the Gospels, believed in and followed him, even though he was a miracle worker. The majority of the Jews chose to remain faithful to the prevailing Jewish concept of the Messiah.

Jesus appeared in a culture where the awaited Messiah was expected to become the warrior king who would rebuild the kingdom of Israel. The concept of a non-political Messiah contravened the belief that the Jews had developed and held about the Messiah over the centuries. It was completely against all expectations of his Jewish audience. So it must have been Jesus who promoted this image and taught that he was non-political. As we have already seen, Jesus must have claimed publicly that he was the Messiah. By doing so he must also have corrected his audience's misconception about the Messiah which had turned him into a national hero rather than a spiritual messenger and reformer.

But is it possible that while distancing himself from any political agenda or role Jesus would still have portrayed himself as king, even if spiritual not earthly, as the Gospels claim? I find this highly unlikely. When trying to change the centuries old perception that the Messiah was going to become the king of the Jews, Jesus would have found this already very difficult task even more so if he called himself king, even if spiritual. Jewish history knew of no spiritual king, as all Jewish kings were earthly. Jesus' efforts to distance himself as the Messiah from any political ambition would have been undermined by any attempt to describe himself as king, albeit spiritual. The Jews would have probably still seen him as a pretender to the throne of David. The Romans also would not have paid much attention to the "spiritual" label, and they would have seen him as a dangerously ambitious Jew.

What about the expressions "kingdom of God" and "kingdom of heaven" that are supposed to have been used by Jesus? Even if Jesus used them, these terms did not suggest that he was royal. Such a kingdom is not one that Jesus would found in which case he would be king. These terms can only refer to a new world that is populated by the righteous which will come into existence after the Day of Resurrection. This is the one universal Day of Judgment that all prophets, including Jesus, spoke about. Jesus could not have spoken about another, earlier heavenly kingdom. In that world, it is God, not Jesus, who is king. Jesus is one of inhabitants of that kingdom.

The Christian image of the Messiah as a *spiritual king* is the result of blending the Jewish concept of the Messiah as an *earthly king* with Jesus' teachings that he was a *spiritual leader* — a prophet from God. Jewish tradition turned the Messiah into a worldly king, the real Messiah stressed that he was not king but a spiritual teacher, and Christian theologians blended the two portraits to present the Messiah as a *spiritual king.*

The earliest believers that Jesus was the Christ came from the Jews of Palestine who had been waiting for the Messiah to save Israel. This firmly established centuries-long Jewish belief about the Messiah stands behind ignoring what Jesus taught about the Christ in the relatively short duration of his mission. The Christians' only *modification* to this detail of the Jewish picture of the Messiah was to say that the Messiah was going to establish his kingdom spiritually not militarily — that is, he was a heavenly king, not an earthly one. This modification was forced on Jesus' followers by his peaceful life and teachings. They had to accept that he was no military man.

What made this distortion to the message of Jesus, and other changes to his teachings, possible is that the New Testament books were written decades after Jesus. The Gospels are the oldest sources of information on the history of Jesus, yet the earliest of these — the Gospel of Mark — was written 30-40 years after Jesus.

This reading of how the concept of Jesus' kingship developed is supported by what the Qur'an says about Jesus the Messiah.

The Non-Royal Qur'anic Messiah

The Qur'an describes Jesus as a "prophet:"

> And when We took a covenant from the prophets; and from you [O Muhammad!]; and from Noah, Abraham, Moses, and Jesus son of Mary. We took from them a solemn covenant. (33.7)

In one of his earliest miracles in which he spoke in the cradle, Jesus told people that he was a prophet: "I am Allah's servant. He has given me the Book and has appointed me a prophet" (19.30).

A "prophet" in the Qur'an is a human being to whom God revealed tidings of the Day of Resurrection and teachings about the true religion. The prophet is charged with communicating this knowledge to people so that they may know the purpose of their creation and act as God wants them to do. Biblical figures such as Adam, Solomon, David, Moses, Zechariah, John, and many others were all prophets. Significantly, the Gospels contain over 20 passages in which people call Jesus "prophet" or he calls himself so:

> And the crowds said, "This is the prophet Jesus, from Nazareth of Galilee." (Matt. 21:11)

> And Jesus said to them, "A prophet is not without honor, except in his hometown and among his relatives and in his own household." (Mark

6:4)

The Qur'an also calls Jesus a "messenger":

> The Messiah son of Mary was no other than a messenger before whom [similar] messengers passed away. (5.75)
>
> Then We made Our messengers to follow in their (Noah and Abraham) footsteps, and followed them up with Jesus son of Mary. (57.27)

The Qur'an also states that the angels described Jesus to Mary when she was given the news about his birth as a "messenger to the Children of Israel" (3.49). Jesus is also quoted as having told the Jews that he was a "messenger of Allah to you" (61.6).

The term "messenger" is related to "prophet" but it has a rather broader sense. It denotes anyone that God sends on a mission, such as delivering a message or performing a particular task. Another difference between "prophet" and "messenger" is that the former is used only for human beings, whereas a messenger may or may not be a human being — for instance, he may be an angel.

Jesus said that he was a prophet with a message from God. His message was a continuation of the message of previous messengers, which is why God said that He "followed them up with Jesus son of Mary" and sent him to confirm the Torah:

> I have come to confirm that which was revealed before me of the Torah, and to make lawful some of that which was forbidden to you [O Children of Israel]. I have come to you with a sign from your Lord, so keep your duty to Allah and obey me. (3.50)

This verse also shows that one aspect of Jesus' mission was to change some *behavioral* but not *doctrinal* laws of the Torah. God did that by revealing to Jesus a book called the "Injīl":

> And He shall teach him (Jesus) the Book, Wisdom, The Torah, and the Injīl. (3.48)

Finally, Jesus' mission also included bringing the good news about the future prophet Muhammad:

> And when Jesus son of Mary said: "O Children of Israel! I am a messenger of Allah to you, confirming that which was revealed before me of the Torah, and bringing good news about a messenger who will come after me, whose name is Aḥmad." But when he came to them with clear proofs, they said: "This is clear magic." (61.6)

We have discussed the "Injīl" in more detail elsewhere (Fatoohi, 2007: 357-388).

So Jesus came to reform the religion that was taught by the earlier prophets and which had been distorted by the Jewish theologians over the centuries. His mission was spiritual and similar to that of the prophets who came before him. Jesus never claimed or wanted to be a king of the Jews or any other people. Messengers in the Qur'an do not have political ambitions, although playing political or military roles may be required for the fulfillment of their messages, as happened, for instance, with Moses, David, and Muhammad. The Jewish image of the Messiah as someone who was expected to reestablish Israel is incompatible with the function of messengers in the Qur'an. Messengers may be sent to a particular nation to guide them to the right path, but they are never sent to exalt an *ethnic* nation over others or lead them to mundane glory.

The distortion that the concept of Messiah had been subjected to, making it a political title, probably made Jesus more cautious when using it, to avoid any possible misunderstanding of his mission by the authorities. He probably stressed more his equally significant titles of God's "messenger" and "prophet." Far from claiming to be king, he must have repeatedly and persistently denied any claim to kingship.

6

A Second Coming for an Unfulfilled Kingdom

We saw in the previous chapter that the early Christians' portrayal of Jesus as a spiritual king had no basis in his teachings but was inspired by the former religion of those converts, Judaism. Another aspect of this influence can be seen in the New Testament's claim that the establishment of the "kingdom of God/heaven" was *imminent,* as the Jews believed that the Messiah would found his kingdom during his lifetime. The adherence of the early Christians to their Jewish beliefs resulted in their development of one of the most fundamental Christian beliefs: Jesus' second coming.

The Need to Bring Jesus Back

Matthew declared the imminence of the kingdom of heaven through John the Baptist:

> In those days John the Baptist came preaching in the wilderness of Judea, "Repent, for the kingdom of heaven is at hand." For this is he who was spoken of by the prophet Isaiah when he said, "The voice of one crying in the wilderness: 'Prepare the way of the Lord; make his paths straight.'" (Matt. 3:1-3)

Mark and Matthew also attribute this claim to Jesus:

> Now after John was arrested, Jesus came into Galilee, proclaiming the gospel of God, and saying, "The time is fulfilled, and the kingdom of God is at hand; repent and believe in the gospel." (Mark 1:14-15)

> From that time Jesus began to preach, saying, "Repent, for the kingdom of heaven is at hand." (Matt. 4:17)

> These twelve Jesus sent out, instructing them, "Go nowhere among the Gentiles and enter no town of the Samaritans, but go rather to the lost sheep of the house of Israel. And proclaim as you go, saying, 'The kingdom of heaven is at hand.'" (Matt. 10:5-7)

The third Synoptist, Luke, also states that Joseph of Arimathea, who is claimed to have buried Jesus after his crucifixion, was also expecting the kingdom of God during his lifetime:

> Now there was a man named Joseph, from the Jewish town of Arimathea. He was a member of the council, a good and righteous man,

who had not consented to their decision and action; and he was looking
for the kingdom of God. (Luke 23:50-51)

But there was a serious problem with portraying the founding of the
Messianic kingdom as imminent.

Jesus was a very low-key figure who had very little impact on
Palestine and its Jewish population during his lifetime. When Jesus left
this world, and for many years afterward, his followers remained a small
group, seen by most Jews as a misguided sect. It was clear that the world
that Jesus left behind was no different from the one he came to.
Furthermore, the Roman political and Jewish theocratic authorities that
controlled Palestine before Jesus were still there after him. The Roman
heathens were still ruling the Jews, and the high priest and the Jewish
legal council known as the "Sanhedrin" continued to manage all religious
affairs in the holy land. The lives and beliefs of the overwhelming
majority of the Jews did not change at all because of his coming. In fact,
Jesus was such a minor figure that a plot was quickly put together to have
him crucified after a summary trial.

Jesus' disappointed followers had then to reconcile an undeniable fact
and a strongly held belief. The difficult fact was that Jesus' kingdom
never materialized and his peaceful life did not include any royal
achievement. In fact, the way they thought it ended reflected
powerlessness of a commoner rather than authority of a royal. The belief,
which originated from their Jewish tradition, was that the Messiah was
going to establish a kingdom and that this was going to happen as soon
as he comes.

The early Christian theologians dealt with this apparent contradiction
by introducing the concept of the "second coming" of Jesus. According to
this modified version of the original Jewish belief about the Messiah, the
kingdom of God would not be founded in the Messiah's first coming but
when he returns. In Judaism, the savior Messiah would come to the
world once.

Of course, Jesus' return had to be imminent for the belief in the
imminence of the Messianic kingdom to continue to hold true. We can
see indeed the belief in the imminence of the second coming in the New
Testament. In the earliest known Christian document, which was written
about two decades after Jesus, we learn that the Christians of
Thessalonica in Macedonia were confounded by the death of fellow
Christians who were expecting to witness the establishment of the
kingdom of God in their lifetime. This prompted Paul to write to them to
reassure them that the believers who had already died would be brought
back to life when Jesus comes back to found the kingdom of heaven. This

was a clever workaround for the problem that the arrival of the eagerly expected kingdom of God was seen to have become late:

> But we do not want you to be uninformed, brothers, about those who are asleep, that you may not grieve as others do who have no hope. For since we believe that Jesus died and rose again, even so, through Jesus, God will bring with him those who have fallen asleep. For this we declare to you by a word from the Lord, that we who are alive, who are left until the coming of the Lord, will not precede those who have fallen asleep. For the Lord himself will descend from heaven with a cry of command, with the voice of an archangel, and with the sound of the trumpet of God. And the dead in Christ will rise first. Then we who are alive, who are left, will be caught up together with them in the clouds to meet the Lord in the air, and so we will always be with the Lord. (1 The. 4:13-17)

We have other passages in the Gospels stating that Jesus said that his advent was going to be during the lifetime of his own generation (also Matt. 24:34; Luke 21:32):

> Truly, I say to you, this generation will not pass away until all these things take place. (Mark 13:30)

Jesus confirmed that his second coming would happen during the lifetime of his audience in an earlier speech to a crowd including his disciples, according to Mark, or to his disciples only, according to Matthew (16:24-28) and Luke (9:23-27):

> Truly, I say to you, there are some standing here who will not taste death until they see the kingdom of God after it has come with power. (Mark 9:1)

While the Evangelists make Jesus himself announce his second coming, they said that he also did not know its precise time (also Matt. 24:36):

> But concerning that day or that hour, no one knows, not even the angels in heaven, nor the Son, but only the Father. Be on guard, keep awake. For you do not know when the time will come. (Mark 13:32-33)

The fact that Jesus' advent had no specific date meant that the concept of it being *imminent* could persist. This unknown imminence combined with Jesus' alleged lack of knowledge of when he would come back were also convenient in explaining Jesus' failed predictions that his advent was going to be during the lifetime of his own generation.

Many scholars (e.g. Sanders, 1995: 95) think that the references to the imminent arrival of the kingdom of God in the New Testament reflect Jesus' own belief. They think that he believed that God was going to intervene and bring about a radical change to the world. I disagree with this view which I think is a consequence of the wrong assumption that Jesus viewed his messiahship in the same way the Jews had understood it. Like the concept of the second coming itself, the imminence of Jesus' alleged return reflected the belief of the early Christians not the Christ.

The Dangerous Politics of the Messiah's Awaited Coming

The coming of the Jewish Messiah and the second coming of the Christian Messiah are not only religious concepts, but they have political dimensions that have had and continue to have an enormous impact on the modern world.

According to the Old Testament, the kingdom that David established in the holy land, which is dated to the 10th century BCE, consisted of the descendants of Jacob, who was also called Israel. These twelve tribes are named after 10 of Jacob's sons and 2 of his grandsons. After the death of David's son Solomon, the kingdom split into two separate states. The southern kingdom of Judea, whose capital was Jerusalem, was occupied by the tribes of Judah and Benjamin. The northern kingdom of Israel, which took Samaria as its capital, was occupied by the other ten tribes. When king Hoshea revolted against the new Assyrian king Shalmaneser V, the latter besieged Israel for three years. Shortly after Shalmaneser's death, around 721 BCE, Samaria fell to his successor, Sargon II. The Assyrian king took Israel's inhabitants captive and scattered them. This is what the Bible has to say about this event:

> In the fourth year of King Hezekiah, which was the seventh year of Hoshea son of Elah, king of Israel, Shalmaneser king of Assyria came up against Samaria and besieged it, and at the end of three years he took it. In the sixth year of Hezekiah, which was the ninth year of Hoshea king of Israel, Samaria was taken. The king of Assyria carried the Israelites away to Assyria and put them in Halah, and on the Habor, the river of Gozan, and in the cities of the Medes. (2 Kings 18:9-11)

More or less the same fate was awaiting Judea and its people. In 597 BCE, the Babylonian king Nebuchadnezzar II captured Jerusalem and took its prominent people into captivity in Babylon. In a second campaign in 586 BCE he destroyed Jerusalem, including the temple. The Old Testament Book of Jeremiah claims that Nebuchadnezzar II took Jewish captives to Babylon three times, corresponding to 597, 586, and 582 BCE:

> This is the number of the people whom Nebuchadnezzar carried away captive: in the seventh year, 3,023 Judeans; in the eighteenth year of

Nebuchadnezzar he carried away captive from Jerusalem 832 persons; in the twenty-third year of Nebuchadnezzar, Nebuzaradan the captain of the guard carried away captive of the Judeans 745 persons; all the persons were 4,600. (Jer. 52:28-30)

After defeating the Babylonians, the Persian king Cyrus allowed its two captive tribes to return home in 539 BCE and rebuild the temple. The scattered ten tribes of Israel did not have such luck because they had already been assimilated by other peoples and were lost.

The Jews believe that the Messiah *will come* to gather all twelve tribes again in their promised land in Palestine. Christians see this gathering as a sign and requirement for the *second coming* of their Messiah, as they believe that the Messiah *has already come*. This is how Jewish Zionism and Christian Zionism have both found in the establishment of the modern state of Israel a sign, condition, and conducive development for the coming of the Messiah, although they believe that each other's Messiah is false! Strengthening the state of Israel, helping and encouraging Jews from all parts of the world to immigrate to Palestine, and usurping more Palestinian lands became a noble religious duty for the Zionists.

There are few mentions of the twelve tribes in the New Testament. For instance, James addressed his Epistle to "the twelve tribes in the Dispersion" (Jam. 1:1). In Matthew (19:28) we see Jesus tell his disciples the following: "When the Son of Man will sit on his glorious throne, you who have followed me will also sit on twelve thrones, judging the twelve tribes of Israel." Luke (22:30) also has a passage in which Jesus tells his disciples that they would be sitting in his kingdom "on thrones judging the twelve tribes of Israel." These passages imply that the twelve tribes would have been gathered by the time of Jesus' second coming. This is the closest New Testament reference that may link Jesus' second coming to the gathering of the twelve tribes.

For a more detailed discussion of Jesus' second coming, the reader may consult my book *The Mystery of the Historical Jesus* (Fatoohi, 2007: 467-507).

The Unreturning Qur'anic Messiah

As we have already seen, as a prophet like all other prophets, Jesus was not commissioned by God to create an earthly kingdom at his time or later. The concept of a spiritual or heavenly kingdom that is specific to Jesus is absent from the Qur'an. Jesus was sent to call people to follow God and be prepared for the Day of Resurrection. This is basically what all other messengers of God preached. The Messiah of the Qur'an does not represent a culmination of the earlier divine messages. He was surely one of the greatest messengers, but he delivered the same core message that those before him and the one after him, Muhammad, preached. He was not commissioned to establish any special kingdom. He worked hard to bring people to God like all messengers of God did.

We have seen how the concept of Jesus' second coming was developed by Jesus' followers to explain his unexpected failure to deliver what *they* thought the Christ was going to do. It is not surprising, therefore, that the Qur'an does not support the concept of the return of its Messiah, Jesus. The Qur'anic Messiah fulfilled his mission. He did not leave the earth with any unfinished job.

Nevertheless, Muslim scholars have suggested that verses 43.61 and 4.159 talk indirectly about Jesus' return, but it is clear from the convoluted nature of these interpretations and the amount of speculation they employ that such attempts are driven by a prior belief in Jesus' return. There are also a number of sayings that are attributed to Prophet Muhammad that supposedly confirm the concept of the second coming. I have discussed elsewhere in detail how such inauthentic sayings and the fanciful interpretations of Qur'anic verses to support the advent of Jesus are inspired by the Christian belief in this concept (Fatoohi, 2007: 483-491).

But the Christian concept of the second coming was not created completely out of thin air. It was based on Jesus' authentic prediction of the coming of Prophet Muhammad:

> And when Jesus son of Mary said: "O Children of Israel! I am a messenger of Allah to you, confirming that which was revealed before me of the Torah, and bringing good news about a messenger who will come after me, whose name is Aḥmad." But when he came to them with clear proofs, they said: "This is clear magic." (61.6)

Jesus' prophecy of the coming of a different prophet, Muhammad, was changed to become a prophecy about Jesus' return. This also explains the absence of Jesus' prophecy about Muhammad's coming from the New Testament, apart from the garbled passages in the Gospel of John (14:16, 26, 15:26, 16:7) and the First Epistle of John (2:1) about the coming of the "paraclete" (p. 87).

Significantly, the Qur'an does not reject the claim that Jesus was an eschatological figure just to claim that Prophet Muhammad was so. Conversely, the Qur'an is clear that Muhammad's coming would not signal the end of times or have any such eschatological meanings or consequences. We see this clearly, for instance, when the Qur'an mentions Muhammad's future death and clearly implies that life would continue after him as usual:

> Truly you [O Muhammad!] shall die and they too shall die. (39.30) Then, verily, on the Day of Resurrection you shall dispute before your Lord. (39.31)
>
> Muhammad is no more than a messenger before whom messengers have already passed away. Should he die, therefore, or get killed, would you turn back on your heels? He who turns back on his heels will not cause Allah any harm. Allah will reward the grateful. (3.144) No soul can die but by the permission of Allah, according to an appointed time. He who wishes for the reward of this world We will give him of it, and he who wishes for the reward of the last life We will give him of it, and We will reward the grateful. (3.145) How many a prophet with whom many fought yet they did not give way at what befell them in Allah's way, weaken, or surrender. Allah loves the patient. (4.146)

Note also how verse 4.146 likens the experience of Muhammad and his followers to what happened to previous prophets. Again, the Qur'an does not single out Prophet Muhammad or associate him with the end of the world. Even when the Qur'an declares that Muhammad is the *last* prophet, it does not state that the world would end after him:

> Muhammad is not the father of any man among you, but he is the Messenger of Allah and the last of the prophets. Allah knows all things. (33.40)

The Arabic word that I have translated as "last," *khātam*, also means "seal." A seal is like the signature that a message ends with, as Muhammad's mission completed God's message that was delivered through various prophets down the centuries. A seal is also a sign of confirmation, as Muhammad confirmed the message of the previous prophets.

7

Son of King David?

As we saw earlier (pp. 8, 17), The Jews believed that the Messiah was going to be a descendant of David:

> Behold, the days are coming, declares the Lord, when I will raise up for David a righteous Branch, and he shall reign as king and deal wisely, and shall execute justice and righteousness in the land. (Jer. 23:5)

It was essential, therefore, for the Gospel writers to prove that Jesus was a descendant of David to present him as the Messiah.

The Synoptics mention incidents in which people called Jesus the "son of David" (also Luke 18:38):

> And they came to Jericho. And as he was leaving Jericho with his disciples and a great crowd, Bartimaeus, a blind beggar, the son of Timaeus, was sitting by the roadside. And when he heard that it was Jesus of Nazareth, he began to cry out and say, "Jesus, Son of David, have mercy on me!" (Mark 10:46-47)

> And behold, a Canaanite woman from that region came out and was crying, "Have mercy on me, O Lord, Son of David; my daughter is severely oppressed by a demon." (Matt. 15:22)

Matthew and Luke have tried to show that Jesus was a descendant of David in two ways: tracing his genealogy to David and claiming that he came from the city of David. Both of these approaches, however, are fraught with problems.

Jesus mother, Mary, was probably a Levite, as she was a relative of Elizabeth, Zechariah's wife, who was a Levite (Luke 1:5, 36). Yet David was not a descendant of Levi but of another of Jacob's sons, Judah. Thus, it was not possible to link Jesus to David through his mother's genealogy. The two Evangelists who tried to use the genealogy approach to link Jesus to David decided therefore to use the genealogy of Joseph, Mary's fiancé, to show that Jesus descended from David. Matthew (1:1) also links this blood relationship with David with the title Christ as he starts his Gospel with what he describes as "the genealogy of Jesus Christ, the son of David, the son of Abraham." The obvious problem with this attempt is that Matthew and Luke also present Jesus as having been conceived miraculously without the involvement of a man, so he had no blood relationship with Joseph! In reality, then, the Gospels fail to trace Jesus' genealogy to David.

Matthew and Luke's second approach was to try and prove that Jesus came from the same city of David, which the Old Testament identifies as Bethlehem (1 Sam. 16:1). Matthew claimed that Jewish scholars — or at least those whom Herod consulted — believed that the Christ was to be born in Bethlehem:

> And assembling all the chief priests and scribes of the people, he inquired of them where the Christ was to be born. They told him, "In Bethlehem of Judea, for so it is written by the prophet: 'And you, O Bethlehem, in the land of Judah, are by no means least among the rulers of Judah; for from you shall come a ruler who will shepherd my people Israel.'" (Matt. 2:4-6)

Both Matthew and Luke claim that Jesus was born in Bethlehem:

> Now after Jesus was born in Bethlehem of Judea in the days of Herod the king, behold, wise men from the east came to Jerusalem. (Matt. 2:1)

> For unto you is born this day in the city of David a Savior, who is Christ the Lord. (Luke 2:11)

> When the angels went away from them into heaven, the shepherds said to one another, "Let us go over to Bethlehem and see this thing that has happened, which the Lord has made known to us." And they went with haste and found Mary and Joseph, and the baby lying in a manger. (Luke 2:15-16)

Matthew and Luke also agree that Jesus grew up in Nazareth, in Galilee.

Mark agrees with Matthew and Luke in suggesting that Jesus was called the son of David, and he also agrees with the other two Synoptists that Jesus lived in Nazareth:

> In those days Jesus came from Nazareth of Galilee and was baptized by John in the Jordan. (Mark 1:9)

But Mark (6:1) differs from Matthew and Luke as he calls Nazareth Jesus' "hometown," implying that he was born there. Bethlehem actually never features anywhere in Mark's history of Jesus!

Like Mark, John does not cover Jesus' birth or childhood, so there is no explicit reference to their locations. It has two significant passages in which people dismiss Jesus. In the first, a Nathanael sarcastically asks: "Can anything good come out of Nazareth?" (John 1:46); and in the second, Pharisees declare that "no prophet arises from Galilee" (John 7:52). These references, which suggest that Jesus was living in Nazareth, have been taken to mean that John makes Nazareth Jesus' place of birth (e.g. Theissen & Merz, 1999: 164). This understanding is confirmed by a third passage in John that contrasts Bethlehem with Galilee, thus suggesting that the latter, where Nazareth is located, is Jesus' birthplace:

> Others said, "This is the Christ." But some said, "Is the Christ to come from Galilee? Has not the Scripture said that the Christ comes from the offspring of David, and comes from Bethlehem, the village where David was?" (John 7:41-42)

So in the only time in which John mentions Bethlehem, he does so only to say that some rejected Jesus' messiahship on the basis that the scripture said that the Messiah would not come from Galilee but from Bethlehem. John (7:52) confirms this later when people are made to say that "no prophet arises from Galilee." So Mark and John contradict Matthew and Luke as they suggest that Jesus came from Nazareth not Bethlehem. Passage 7:41-42 also suggests that Jesus was not believed to be a son of David!

But the contradictions do not end here. John mentions an earlier incident in which some Jerusalemites controversially claim that the place where the Christ would come from was unknown:

> "Can it be that the authorities really know that this is the Christ? But we know where this man comes from, and when the Christ appears, no one will know where he comes from." So Jesus proclaimed, as he taught in the temple, "You know me, and you know where I come from? But I have not come of my own accord. He who sent me is true, and him you do not know. I know him, for I come from him, and he sent me." (John 7:26-29)

This, clearly, contradict passages we quoted earlier.

Despite the Synoptists' repeated statements about Jesus being the son of David, they report an incident in which Jesus clearly objected to the claim that the Christ was the son of David (Matt. 22:41-46; Luke 20:41-44)! This is Mark's version:

> And as Jesus taught in the temple, he said, "How can the scribes say that the Christ is the son of David? David himself, in the Holy Spirit, declared, 'The Lord said to my Lord, Sit at my right hand, until I put your enemies under your feet.' David himself calls him Lord. So how is he his son?" And the great throng heard him gladly. (Mark 12:35-37)

It may be argued that Jesus was trying to make some theological point here, for instance to emphasize the Christ's superiority to David. But if that is the case then Jesus would have at least solved the puzzle for his audience and not left them questioning what is supposed to be one of the basic facts about the Christ: his descent from David. Jesus would not have helped his audience pick any subtle point he might have wanted to make about the origin of the Christ by presenting them with a difficult puzzle that, at least on the face of it, meant that the Messiah could not have been a son of David. It is significant that in the only instance in which Jesus talks about the Messiah's alleged blood relation to King David, he rejects this link.

The following table summarizes the position of the four Evangelists about various aspects of Jesus' background and relationship to David:

Information	Mark	Matthew	Luke	John
Birthplace	Nazareth	Bethlehem	Bethlehem	Nazareth
Growing-up	Nazareth	Nazareth	Nazareth	Nazareth
Jesus is called "son of David"	Yes	Yes	Yes	No
Jesus' sonship of David is questioned	No	No	No	Yes
Jesus is linked to David by blood	No	Yes	Yes	No
The Christ' coming from Bethlehem is questioned	No	No	No	Yes
Jesus rejects that the Christ is a son of David	Yes	Yes	Yes	No

Matthew and Luke are in line with each other, but Mark has differences with them. John has yet more differences with the three Synoptists. John is so different that he agrees with Mathew and Luke only on that Jesus grew up in Nazareth; he contradicts them on everything else! He does not mention Jesus' sonship of David. This is one example that shows how different the four Gospels are from each other. As I have pointed out:

> The label "Synoptic" should not give the wrong impression that Mark, Matthew, and Luke are consistent with each other... There are numerous disagreements between these three books, and even within each. The common use of the singular term "Gospel" to refer to the four Gospels in the sense of implying that they tell a coherent story is completely misleading. There are different Jesuses in the different Gospels, and there is more than one Jesus in any one Gospel. (Fatoohi, 2007: 22)

Each Gospel was written to reflect certain traditions and perceptions, and there is no reason to suggest that these different sources and drives were always reconcilable. Clearly, they were not.

The Qur'anic Messiah: Son of Mary not Son of David

The Qur'an confirms that Mary's conception of Jesus was virginal. This is clear, for instance, in Mary's reply to Gabriel after hearing the good news that she was going to have a son (also 19.20):

How can I have a child when no human being has touched me? (3.47)

The Qur'anic story of Mary contains many references confirming that Mary's conception of Jesus was not the result of a relationship with a man. It was a unique miraculous conception. Jesus did not have paternal ancestry.

The Qur'an gives very little information about Mary's ancestry. We know that her father was called 'Imrān, as she is called "daughter of 'Imrān" and her mother is referred to as the "wife of 'Imrān":

> And [Allah set forth an example] Mary, daughter of 'Imrān, who guarded her private parts, then We breathed therein of Our spirit. And she believed in the words of her Lord and His Book, and was one of the obedient. (66.12)
>
> When the wife of 'Imrān said: "My Lord! I vow to consecrate to You that which is in my womb, so accept it from me. You are the Hearer, the Knower." (3.35)

The Qur'an also tells us that "the family of 'Imrān" was very special:

> Allah chose Adam, Noah, the family of Abraham, and the family of 'Imrān above all nations (3.33) — offspring, one of the other; and Allah hears and knows all things. (3.34)

Exegetes have understood the four divine acts of choosing as denoting the distinguished qualities of these two individuals and two extended families. Adam was chosen to be the first human being. Noah was elected to survive with his followers the deluge and be the one from whom all prophets descended. The family of Abraham was chosen to have a large number of prophets and in a relatively short period of time, through Isaac, and to produce the last Prophet, Muhammad, through Abraham's other son, Ishmael. The other special family, which is that of 'Imrān, included the two unique figures of Mary and her son Jesus.

Verse 4.34 suggests that these acts of choosing by God should also be understood in terms of the special offspring that each of these individuals or families was given and their belonging to one bloodline. Adam was chosen to be the first human being, and thus the father of the human race, including all prophets. Noah was a great grandfather of Abraham. The family of Abraham was the ancestors of 'Imrān and possibly his wife also. This couple was chosen to have the very special daughter Mary, who was in turn given the unique privilege of becoming the mother of Jesus through a unique miracle.

We learn another piece of information about Mary's ancestry from a verse in which people who knew her call her "sister of Aaron", in the context of denouncing her giving birth to Jesus without marriage:

O Mary! You have come up with a grave thing. (from 19.27) O sister of
Aaron! Your father was not a bad man, and your mother was not an
unchaste woman. (19.28)

One common mistake among Biblical scholars is to understand the
expression "sister of Aaron" as meaning that Mary had a brother called
"Aaron." Noting that "Amram" is called the father of "Aaron and Moses and
Miriam their sister" in the Old Testament Book of Numbers (26:59),
Biblicists argue that the Qur'an confuses Mary, the mother of Jesus and
daughter of 'Imrān, with Miriam, Aaron's sister, whose father was
Amram. They, thus, claim that the Qur'an contains corrupt information
from the Bible (e.g. Tisdall, 1905:150-151). This is rather an act of
confusion by the Biblical writers.

When relating a person to his/her people, the Qur'an describes that
person as *akh* (brother) or *ukht* (sister) of that people. This is one
example:

The people of Noah rejected the messengers (26.105). When their
akhūhum (brother) Noah said to them: "Will you not be dutiful [toward
Allah]?" (26.106)

Thus, "sister of Aaron" means that Mary was a descendant of a famous
grandfather known as "Aaron." Exegetes believe it is prophet Aaron,
Moses' brother. According to the Bible, Aaron did not descend from
David.

There is nothing in the Qur'an that links Jesus to the bloodline of
prophet David. This, clearly, is *negative evidence*. But there is also a very
significant fact that represents positive evidence that the Qur'an does not
link Jesus to David: Jesus is called "son of Mary."

The Qur'an calls Jesus "son of Mary" 23 times. This title occurs 13
times as "Jesus son of Mary" (2.87, 2.53, 5.46, 5.78, 5.110, 5.112, 5.114,
5.117, 19.34, 33.7, 57.27, 61.6, 61.14), 5 times as "the Messiah son of Mary"
(5.17 (twice), 5.72, 5.75, 9.31), 3 times as "the Messiah Jesus son of Mary"
(3.45, 4.157, 4.171), and 2 times with no other name or title (23.50,
43.57). Jesus is also referred to once as "her son," i.e. Mary's son (21.91).
There are two significant observations to make about this title:

(1) The title "son of Mary" is clearly intended to emphasize the fact that
Jesus had no father. It is probably what people called him at the time,
influenced by his unique, miraculous origin. But it cannot mean that
Jesus had an *unknown father*, because it is a title that God also used for
Jesus, not only one used by people who did not know Jesus' father. God
is described as omniscient in the Qur'an, so it cannot be claimed that this
title implies that Jesus' father was unknown. It can only mean that Jesus

had no father.

(2) This title relates Jesus to his mother, so the absence of the title "son of David" is not the result of Jesus not being related to any of his ancestors.

(3) No other prophet or person in the Qur'an is given a title after his mother.

It should also be noted that the Qur'an does not promote any ethnic identification of any prophet. The one significant identity of each of them is that he is a prophet of God.

By Jesus' time, the Jews had already developed the view that the Messiah was going to come to restore Israel. It is natural, therefore, that they made the Messiah a descendant of King David, the warrior king who founded Israel. Christian sources, which present Jesus as the Messiah, are thus keen on stressing his descent from David, as this was seen as a *condition* and *sign* of messiahship by the Jews of the time.

The Qur'an does not support the Jewish military image of the Messiah, so it is natural to expect it to reject describing Jesus a "son of David."

8

Savior?

Both Jewish and Christian sources agree that the Messiah had a salvational role.

For the Jews, the salvation of the royal Messiah is about rescuing them from their heathen rulers and restoring their kingdom. This is why the Gospel accounts of Jesus' crucifixion contain a number of sarcastic remarks by Jesus' opponents about him being the Christ and saving people yet not being able to save himself.

Mark (15:31-32) states that the Jewish leaders derided the crucified Jesus: "He saved others; he cannot save himself. Let the Christ, the King of Israel, come down now from the cross that we may see and believe." Almost the same account is also found in Matthew (27:42), although the title Christ is not used. Luke (23:35) has people who were watching the crucifixion mock Jesus saying: "He saved others; let him save himself, if he is the Christ of God, his Chosen One!" The soldiers told Jesus: "If you are the King of the Jews, save yourself" (Luke 23:37). One of the criminals who were crucified with him also said to Jesus sarcastically: "Are you not the Christ? Save yourself and us" (Luke 23:39).

For the Christians also, the Messiah is a savior. According to Luke, the angel told the shepherds: "Unto you is born this day in the city of David a Savior, who is Christ the Lord" (Luke 2:11). Similarly, while not using the term Christ, John says that the Samaritans were convinced that Jesus was really "the Savior of the world" (John 4:42). But according to the Gospels, Jesus described himself as a spiritual leader who had nothing to do with realizing the Jewish dream of the restoration of Israel, so the salvation he offered was spiritual. This is clearly explained in Matthew (1:21) as an angel told Joseph in a dream about the son that Mary will bear: "You shall call his name Jesus, for he will save his people from their sins." The Gospels say that Jesus taught people how to repent and lead a life that is accepted by God. He told them about God's path, but people are ultimately saved by their own actions.

Luke (24:21) reports that after Jesus' death, two of his disciples disappointedly said that they "had hoped that he was the one to redeem Israel." But this statement can also be seen as meaning *spiritual* redemption. Even the kingdom that he is going to establish in his second coming is spiritual.

Paul also gives Jesus the role of saving people from sin, but he makes Jesus do that in a way that is completely different from what is found anywhere in the Gospels. Paul introduced the doctrine of the "atonement." He says that as a result of the sin of their father, Adam, all people are born in a state of sin. Sin means perishing for good after death. To earn eternal life, people need salvation. God offered man salvation by making the resurrection of his son, Jesus, signify the hope to be freed from sin and to attain eternal life: "For just as in Adam all die, so also in Christ all will be made alive" (1 Cor. 15:22). This salvation is attained by those who believe in Jesus as their savior. The atonement, thus, denotes the reconciliation between God and man that is brought about by the death and resurrection of Jesus.

Although atonement is a strictly Pauline doctrine that is not found in the Gospels, which are also the oldest surviving biographies of Jesus, it has become one of the most important doctrines of Christianity, if not the most important one. This attests to the unparalleled influence that Paul managed to muster, even though he never met Jesus and converted to Christianity several years after Jesus.

The Qur'anic Messiah: No Unique Savior

The Qur'an presents Jesus as a messenger and prophet, albeit a special one who was conceived by a unique miracle and performed many impressive miracles. Like any prophet, he showed people the right path to God and invited them to follow it, leading by example. By doing this, he helped his followers attain salvation. This salvational role is what every prophet was commanded by God to do. It was not unique to Jesus.

Paul's view that Jesus came to save people from the original sin is also rejected by the Qur'an which describes Jesus as a prophet. A prophet is a messenger whose duty is to deliver God's commandments to people about what they must believe in and how they should live. The prophet himself is not the focus of the message; he is only the messenger who delivers. It is the responsibility of the individual to believe the prophet's divine message. The prophet could not do anything that would save people in the same way the crucifixion and resurrection of Jesus are supposed to do. Every prophet guided people to God, but without the involvement of any form of redemption. Significantly, this role of the prophet in the Qur'an has a lot of similarity with how the Gospels, not Paul's letters, describe Jesus' life and his efforts to guide people to salvation.

Jesus' salvational role is further distorted in the New Testament by the confused picture of him being not only a man but also having divine qualities. Paul believed that Jesus was a human incarnation of God. But the most striking deification of Jesus is found in the Gospel of John. This Evangelist' portrayal of Jesus' divinity has greatly influenced how Christianity saw Jesus even though it conflicted with his image in the Synoptic Gospels. John all but removed any difference between Jesus the son of God and the father himself. This is one passage that attributes to Jesus words to this effect:

> Whoever has seen me has seen the Father. How can you say, "Show us the Father"? Do you not believe that I am in the Father and the Father is in me? The words that I say to you I do not speak on my own authority, but the Father who dwells in me does his works. Believe me that I am in the Father and the Father is in me, or else believe on account of the works themselves. (John 14:9-11)

Jesus is said to have announced his preexistence and coexistence with God:

> I glorified you on earth, having accomplished the work that you gave me to do. And now, Father, glorify me in your own presence with the glory that I had with you before the world existed. (John 17:4-5)

The elevation of Jesus to divinity provided Christian writers and theologians with the explanation and justification for the alleged uniqueness of his salvational function. The Jewish Messiah, of course, was not divine but a human being.

Attributing divinity to Jesus is completely rejected by the Qur'an. The Qur'anic Jesus is a human prophet of God who never claimed to be divine, who preached in a monotheistic society that did not believe in more than one God, and who was deified only after he was gone (Fatoohi, 2007: 287-312). This is one verse that confirms that the Messiah was a messenger like those God sent before him, his mother was a righteous woman, and both, like any other human being, had to eat their daily food to survive:

> The Messiah son of Mary was no other than a messenger before whom [similar] messengers passed away, and his mother was a saintly woman. They used to eat food [like other human beings]. See how We make the revelations clear to them (the Christians), and see how they are deluded! (5.75)

9

Miracle Worker

The four Gospels report a variety of miracles that Jesus performed. His miracles may be divided into four categories: **healings, nature miracles, prophecies**, and **clairvoyance miracles**. The most reported type of miracles is healing. Healing miracles may in turn be subdivided into **healings of diseases, exorcisms of devils**, and **resurrections of dead people**.

The table below shows the number of Jesus' miracles that each Gospel reports:

Miracle Category		Mark	Matthew	Luke	John
Healing	Diseases	14	18	16	4
	Exorcisms	5	4	4	0
	Resurrections	0	0	1	1
	Total	**19**	**22**	**21**	**5**
Nature		6	6	4	4
Prophecies		5	5	3	0
Clairvoyance		1	2	1	1
Total		**31**	**35**	**29**	**10**

All four Evangelists claim that the Christ was understood to be a miracle worker: "Yet many of the people believed in him. They said, 'When the Christ appears, will he do more signs than this man has done?'" (John 7:31). Luke suggests that Jesus was recognized as the Christ *because he performed miracles*:

> Now when the sun was setting, all those who had any who were sick with various diseases brought them to him, and he laid his hands on every one of them and healed them. And demons also came out of many, crying, "You are the Son of God!" But he rebuked them and would not allow them to speak, because they knew that he was the Christ. (Luke 4:40-41)

Bringing Lazarus back to life made his sister call Jesus the Christ (John 11:17-27). Elsewhere John states that Jesus' miracles prove that he is the Messiah:

> Now Jesus did many other signs in the presence of the disciples, which are not written in this book; but these are written so that you may believe

that Jesus is the Christ, the Son of God, and that by believing you may have life in his name. (John 20:30-31)

The disciple Peter confessed that Jesus was "the Christ of God" after the miracle of feeding 5,000 people (Luke 9:20). John (4:25-29) also tells us that a Samaritan woman who was the subject of one of Jesus' clairvoyance miracles accepted that he was the Messiah:

> So the woman left her water jar and went away into town and said to the people, "Come, see a man who told me all that I ever did. Can this be the Christ?" (John 4:28-29)

Matthew (11:2-5) and Luke report another incident in which Jesus clearly stresses to disciples of John the Baptist that his miracles attested to his status as the awaited Messiah, although the term "Messiah" is only implied:

> The disciples of John reported all these things to him. And John, calling two of his disciples to him, sent them to the Lord, saying, "Are you the one who is to come, or shall we look for another?" And when the men had come to him, they said, "John the Baptist has sent us to you, saying, 'Are you the one who is to come, or shall we look for another?'" In that hour he healed many people of diseases and plagues and evil spirits, and on many who were blind he bestowed sight. And he answered them, "Go and tell John what you have seen and heard: the blind receive their sight, the lame walk, lepers are cleansed, and the deaf hear, the dead are raised up, the poor have good news preached to them." (Luke 7:18-22)

This passage seems to utilize an Isaiah (35:4-6) prophecy, whose fulfillment the Dead Sea Scrolls place at the time of the Messiah (Theissen & Merz, 1999: 212), and other Isaiah passages:

> Say to those who have an anxious heart, "Be strong; fear not! Behold, your God will come with vengeance, with the recompense of God. He will come and save you." Then the eyes of the blind shall be opened, and the ears of the deaf unstopped; then shall the lame man leap like a deer, and the tongue of the mute sing for joy. For waters break forth in the wilderness, and streams in the desert. (Isa. 35:4-6)

> Your dead shall live; their bodies shall rise. You who dwell in the dust, awake and sing for joy! For your dew is a dew of light, and the earth will give birth to the dead. (Isa. 26:19)

> In that day the deaf shall hear the words of a book, and out of their gloom and darkness the eyes of the blind shall see. The meek shall obtain fresh joy in the Lord, and the poor among mankind shall exult in the Holy One of Israel. (Isa. 29:18-19)

> The Spirit of the Lord God is upon me, because the Lord has anointed me to bring good news to the poor; he has sent me to bind up the

brokenhearted, to proclaim liberty to the captives, and the opening of the prison to those who are bound. (Isa. 61:1)

In keeping with his keen interest in representing Jesus' life as the fulfillment of Old Testament prophecies, Matthew reminds his readers that Jesus' miracles fulfilled a specific prophecy in Isaiah:

That evening they brought to him many who were oppressed by demons, and he cast out the spirits with a word and healed all who were sick. This was to fulfill what was spoken by the prophet Isaiah: "He took our illnesses and bore our diseases." (Matt. 8:16-17)

The prophecy in question is part of this passage: "Surely he has borne our griefs and carried our sorrows; yet we esteemed him stricken, smitten by God, and afflicted" (Isa. 53:4).

Matthew (26:68) says that after being physically attacked by the Sanhedrin during his summary trial, Jesus was sarcastically asked by his abusers to "prophesy" who hit him. This also suggests that the Christ was expected to have paranormal powers, including the ability to know the names of people whom he had not met before.

The same connection between the Christ and miracles is met in Mark's scene of the crucifixion, when the chief priests and the scribes mocked Jesus saying: "Let the Christ, the King of Israel, come down now from the cross that we may see and believe" (Mark 15:32).

Matthew reports five different instances in which people called Jesus the "Son of David," meaning the Messiah, because of his miracles (Matt. 9:27, 12:23, 15:22, 20:30, 21:15). One of these incidents (Matt. 20:30) is found in Mark (10:47) and Luke (18:38) also.

Despite what the Gospels say, Jews in the first century, professor Sanders explains, never linked the title Messiah to performing miracles or sonship of God:

The early Christians thought that Jesus was the Messiah, the Son of God, *and* a miracle-worker. This has led many modern Christians to think that first-century Jews looked for a Messiah who performed miracles, and that Jesus' contemporaries would conclude that a miracle-worker was the Messiah. This view is incorrect. The few references to a coming Messiah in Jewish literature do not depict him as a miracle-worker. There was no expectation of a coming Son of God at all. Like other ancient people, Jews believed in miracles but did not think that the ability to perform them proved exalted status. The combination of the titles "Messiah" and "Son of God" with the ability to perform miracles is a Christian one, the result of assigning both titles to Jesus, who was known in his day as a miracle-worker. (Sanders, 1995: 132-133)

Even if the Messiah was not expected to perform miracles, Jesus' miracles must have supported his claims, one of which is that he was the

Christ. Jesus performed miracles in front of not only individuals but also large numbers of people. The largest reported number of witnesses of one of Jesus' miracles is 5,000 men (Mark 6:44; Luke 9:14; John 6:10) — a figure to which Matthew (14:21) adds an unspecified number of women and children.

Unsurprisingly, then, the news about Jesus' miracles reached many places (e.g. Mark 1:45, 7:36; Matt. 9:26; Luke 4:37, 5:15, 8:39). At once, Jesus' "fame spread everywhere throughout all the surrounding region of Galilee" (Mark 1:28), reaching Herod in Judea (Mark 6:14), and "throughout all Syria" (Matt. 4:24). Luke (23:8) claims that "when Herod saw Jesus, he was very glad, for he had long desired to see him, because he had heard about him, and he was hoping to see some sign done by him." This publicity was greatly helped by the fact that Jesus performed miracles in various towns and villages and the countryside (Mark 1:38-39, 6:56; Matt. 9:35, 11:21-23).

Furthermore, Jesus asked people to publicize his miracles. When a man he healed wanted to go with him he ordered him to go home and tell people how he drove a demon out of him (also Luke 8:39):

> As he was getting into the boat, the man who had been possessed with demons begged him that he might be with him. And he did not permit him but said to him, "Go home to your friends and tell them how much the Lord has done for you, and how he has had mercy on you." And he went away and began to proclaim in the Decapolis how much Jesus had done for him, and everyone marveled. (Mark 5:18-20)

When Pharisees warned Jesus that he should disappear because Herod wanted to kill him, he told them to go and tell Herod that he was casting out demons and performing healings (Luke 13:31-32).

The Gospels, nevertheless, also suggest that Jesus tried to keep some of his miracles secret (e.g. Mark 1:44, 5:43, 7:36; Matt. 8:4, 9:30; Luke 5:14, 8:56). These statements contradict the general picture that the Gospels give of Jesus performing miracles in front of anyone and everywhere, clearly seeking publicity to support his mission.

It is also worth mentioning here that Luke suggests that some people wondered whether John the Baptist was the Christ merely on the basis of his virtuous teachings (Luke 3:15). It is no surprise that people associated the Messiah with calling people to righteous conduct, but it is highly unlikely that the Messiah would have been identified on the basis of spiritual preaching only. Jesus' miracles must have played a major role in him being accepted by some Jews as the awaited Messiah. Jesus' miracles in the Gospels are discussed in detail in my book *The Mystery of the Historical Jesus* (Fatoohi, 2007: 313-356).

The Miracle-Working Qur'anic Messiah

As mentioned earlier, Jesus' messiahship was accepted by only a small number of Jews. The Gospels' image of Jesus being seen, heard, and surrounded by thousands and thousands of followers wherever he went is unhistorical. He was followed and witnessed by a small number of people, so his miracles also had a small number of witnesses. The Qur'an does not endorse anywhere the Gospels' unhistorical claim about Jesus' huge popularity.

The Qur'an describes Jesus as an exceptional miracle worker. It attributes to him eight different kinds of miracles, the first of which happened when Jesus was still an infant in the cradle:

(1) **Speaking in infancy**: Jesus was able to speak when he was still in the cradle:

> Lo! When Allah said: "O Jesus son of Mary! Remember My favor on you and on your mother, that I have supported you with the Spirit of Holiness, [making you] speak to people in the cradle and when middle-aged." (from 5.110)

He first spoke immediately after his birth, when he consoled and reassured his upset mother who had left her people after becoming pregnant without marriage:

> And the pangs of childbirth drove her to the trunk of a palm tree. She said: "I wish I had died before this and had become someone totally forgotten!" (19.23) Then he called her from beneath her: "Do not grieve! Your Lord has placed a rivulet beneath you. (19.24) And shake the trunk of the palm tree toward you, and it will let fall fresh dates upon you. (19.25) So eat, drink, and be consoled. If you meet any human being, say: 'I have vowed a fast to God, so I will not speak today to any person.'" (19.26)

Some exegetes of the Qur'an have suggested that the speaker in 19.24 was not Jesus but Gabriel, and others have only identified it as an angel. I believe that the speaker is Jesus for three main reasons:

(i) From the second part of verse 21 through verse 34 the masculine pronoun clearly refers to Jesus. Verse 24 falls in the middle of those verses, and there is no indication that the referent of the pronoun has changed.

(ii) The speaker called Mary "from beneath her." This physical location must mean that the newborn starts speaking as soon as she gave birth to him. Significantly, when the Qur'an reports that someone is spoken to by Gabriel or an angel, it does not specify a physical location for the speaker (see for instance when the angels called Zechariah (3.39)).

(iii) When Mary went back to her people carrying her son, they accused her of giving birth to an illicit child. Her only response was to point to the infant to speak:

> Then she brought him to her people, carrying him. They said: "O Mary! You have come up with a grave thing. (19.27) O sister of Aaron! Your father was not a bad man, and your mother was not an unchaste woman." (19.28) Then she pointed to him. They said: "How can we talk to one who is a child in the cradle?" (19.29)

How did Mary know that the infant in the cradle can speak? It is true that the angels had told her that her son would speak in the cradle:

> When the angels said: "O Mary! Allah gives you the good news of a Word from Him, whose name is the Messiah, Jesus son of Mary, who is illustrious in this world and the hereafter, and who is one of those brought near [to Allah]. (3.45) He shall speak to people in the cradle and when middle-aged, and he shall be one of the righteous." (3.46)

But this good news was delivered some nine months before Mary asked her people to speak to her son. It is extremely unlikely that Mary thought that she could ask for this miracle to happen for the first time and at will when she took her son to her people. It is far more likely that she had already heard the infant speak so she knew that she could ask her people to speak to him.

Also, why would Mary make this connection between her fasting from speech and Jesus' speaking on her behalf? She did that because it was Jesus who asked her to fast from talking to people.

There is one last point that we need to consider. God mentioned that Jesus would speak to people when he is still "in the cradle" (3.46, 5.110), so does this mean that he could not have spoken as soon as he was born? The answer is no. The expression "in the cradle" denotes the fact that Jesus was still a little baby. It does not mean that he could speak *only* if he was physically in a cradle! After all, verse 19.27 does not say that when Jesus spoke to his mother's people he was physically in a cradle. It only says that she was carrying him.

Also, note the response of Mary's people to her suggestion that they should speak to Jesus: "How can we talk to one who is a child in the cradle?" They clearly used the expression "in the cradle" to argue that he was still a very little baby, not to specify where he was laying. Finally, there are two verses in which Jesus' speaking in the cradle is mentioned in the following expression "in the cradle and when middle-aged" (3.46; 5.110). Clearly, the term "in the cradle," like "middle-aged," is used here to denote the age of the child not the fact that he was physically in the cradle.

Back to the account of the miracle, as his mother was fasting from speaking to people, the infant Jesus leaped to her defense, stunning her attackers as he miraculously spoke about his unique nature:

> He said: "I am Allah's servant. He has given me the Book and has appointed me a prophet. (19.30) He has made me blessed wherever I may be. He has enjoined upon me prayer and almsgiving so long as I remain alive. (19.31) And [He has made me] kind to my mother and has not made me arrogant or wretched. (19.32) Peace is on me the day I was born, the day I shall die, and the day I shall be raised alive." (19.33)

Jesus' speaking while still an infant is not mentioned in the canonical Gospels. Interestingly, Matthew and Luke contain no alternative incident or explanation as to why people did not think that Jesus was an illicit child, which would have led them to subject Mary to the Jewish capital punishment of stoning. But this miracle is found in the apocryphal Arabic Gospel of the Infancy, which derives its names from the fact that it survives only in Arabic, but it is also known as the First Gospel of the Infancy of Jesus Christ:

> Jesus spoke even when he was in the cradle, and said to his mother: "Mary, I am Jesus the Son of God, that word, which you did bring forth according to the declaration of the angel Gabriel to you, and my father has sent me for the salvation of the world." (AraIn. 1:2-3)

Jesus is shown here telling his mother that he was Jesus her son whom she gave birth to according to the news that she received from Gabriel. But Mary already knew this, so there was no reason for him to say it! The miracle is poorly weaved into the fabric of the story. In the Qur'an, there is a clear reason as to why Jesus spoke to his mother's people and why he said those words, but the equivalent passage in the apocryphal gospel is clearly out-of-context.

This is an example of a miracle that the apocryphal writer, or his source, was aware of but did not know correctly its context so the report ended up being poorly integrated into the story. It is an instance of what I have called "contextual displacement." The latter denotes a special kind of *textual corruption* in Jewish and Christian writings where "a character, event, or statement appears in one context in the Qur'an and in a different context in other sources." Contextual displacements are the result of "the Bible's editors moving figures, events, and statements from their correct, original contexts" (Fatoohi, 2007: 39).

Note also how Jesus' authentic declaration of his *servanthood to God* was turned into an announcement about his *sonship of God*. His role as a *prophet* was also changed to *savior*.

(2) **Paranormal precociousness**: The miracles above are not only of an infant speaking, but they are equally about the nature of his speech. Jesus spoke with the kind of wisdom, knowledge, and logic that can only be expected from well educated adults. He astonished people not only because he spoke in the cradle, but also by what he had to say, i.e. his precociousness. These are two miracles, not one.

Jesus' precociousness should not be surprising if we note his following words: "He has given me the Book and has appointed me a prophet" (19.30). They reveal that he was given the special knowledge of the Book and was made a prophet while he was still an infant.

(3) **Creating figures of birds from clay and then giving them life**: Jesus' ability to create birds from clay and then turn them into living birds is mentioned twice in two different verses that mention most of Jesus' miracles. The first occurs in Jesus' following speech to his people:

> I have come to you with a sign from your Lord. I create for you out of clay the figures of birds, then I breathe into it [the clay], and it becomes birds by Allah's permission. (from 3.49)

The second is found in God's reminder to Jesus of his favors to him:

> And that you create out of clay the figures of birds by My permission, then you breath into them and they become birds by My permission. (from 5.110)

The miracle of creating figures of birds from clay and then breathing life into them is missing from the canonical Gospels, but the apocryphal gospels have a number of different and more detailed versions of this miracle. The Arabic Gospel of Infancy (15:2-4) talks about Jesus making clay into shapes of asses, oxen, birds, and other figures, and making them move forward and backward at his command. It also states that Jesus made the figures of birds and sparrows out of clay, and made them fly, drink, and eat (AraIn. 15:6). This gospel (19:16-19), the Infancy Gospel of Thomas (2), and the Gospel of Pseudo-Matthew (27) report another miracle in which Jesus created 12 sparrows of clay and at the clap of his hands he made them fly and chirp.

(4) **Healing blindness**: These verses mention Jesus' ability to heal the blind:

> I heal the blind person and the albino. (from 3.49)

> And [you] heal the blind person and the albino by My permission. (from 5.110)

Exegetes and linguists are not in complete agreement about what type of blindness is meant by the Qur'anic Arabic word *akmah*, which I have translated as "blind." It probably signified more than one kind of blindness.

The healing of blindness is also mentioned in the canonical Gospels (Mark 8:22-25, 10:46-52; Matt. 9:27-30, 12:22, 15:30, 20:29-34, 21:14; Luke 18:35-42; John 9:1-7).

(5) Healing albinism or serious skin diseases: Verses 3.49 and 5.110 mention Jesus' miracles of healing albinism. Like *akmah*, the word *abraṣ*, which I have rendered as "albino," probably denotes more than one type of skin disease. The seriousness of blindness as a disability and the impressive nature of the other miracles mentioned in these verses suggest that *abraṣ* is used in the Qur'an for people with serious skin diseases.

Curing albinism is not mentioned in the Gospels, but healing leprosy is (Mark 1:40-42; Matt. 8:2-3; Luke 5:12-13, 17:12-14).

(6) Raising the dead: One of Jesus' impressive miracles is raising dead people, but the Qur'an does not give details beyond mentioning the miracle:

> I raise the dead, by Allah's permission. (from 3.49)
> And that you raise the dead by My permission. (from 5.110)

There are two instances of raising a dead person in the canonical Gospels. Luke (7:12-15) has a story about Jesus bringing back to life the son of a widow, and John (11:38-44) mentions raising Lazarus from the dead.

(7) Knowing what people ate and stored in the privacy of their homes: One verse states that Jesus had the miraculous ability to know what people ate and stored in the privacy of their homes:

> I tell you what you eat and what you store in your houses. (from 3.49)

The canonical Gospels attribute to Jesus three instances of clairvoyance, but they do not include this specific one. In one instance, Jesus knew that a girl was in a coma not dead (Mark 5:22-42; Matt. 9:18-25; Luke 8:41-55). In the second, he talked of a fish that had a coin hidden in its mouth (Matt. 17:24-27). Finally, he was able to tell that a Samaritan woman whom he had not met before had five husbands and a lover (John 4:7-29).

(8) Bringing down from heaven a table of food: Jesus brought from heaven a table of food in response to a request by his companions:

> Lo! When I inspired the companions: "Believe in Me and in My messenger." They said: "We believe. Bear witness that we are Muslims." (5.111) Lo! When the companions said: "O Jesus son of Mary! Can your Lord send down for us a table of food from heaven?" He said: "Observe your duty to Allah, if you are true believers." (5.112) They said: "We wish

to eat of it, have our hearts be at ease, know that you have spoken the truth to us, and be witnesses to it (the table)". (5.113) Jesus son of Mary said: "O Allah our Lord! Send down for us from heaven a table of food, that it may be a feast for the first and the last of us, and a sign from You. Give us sustenance; You are the best of Sustainers." (5.114) Allah said: "I shall send it down for you, so whoever of you disbelieves afterward I will punish him with a torment wherewith I do not inflict on anyone among all the nations." (5.115)

While the companions asked for a table of food from heaven, Jesus' request for it to be a "feast" (*'idan*) means that he asked for plenty of food, as during feasts people celebrate with a lot of food. Also, while the companions asked for a table of food that *they* can eat from, Jesus prayed for one that would feed *all of the present people*, which probably means that people other than his companions were present. So the miracle that Jesus performed was even greater than what the companions asked to see. I have discussed elsewhere in detail how the Gospel stories of the Last Supper (Mark 14:16-26; Matt. 26:18-30; Luke 22:10-38; John 13:1-17:26) and the challenge to Jesus to show a sign from heaven — which, according to John (6:28-33), was about bringing food from heaven — are corrupted versions of the real event of the miracle of the table of food from heaven that the Qur'an recounts (Fatoohi, 2007: 353-355).

Jesus' miracles attested to his claims about his mission and identity, including being the Messiah, which is why God calls them "clear proofs":

And We gave Moses the Book and followed him with a succession of messengers; and We gave Jesus son of Mary *clear proofs*. (from 2.87)

Those are the messengers. We conferred on some more favor than on others. Among them there are some to whom Allah spoke, while some of them He exalted [above others] in degree; and We gave Jesus son of Mary *clear proofs*. (from 2.253)

There is no indication that miracles in general or Jesus' specific miracles characterized the Messiah in particular. Miracles in the Qur'an are attributed to a number of prophets. But Jesus' miracles were proofs not only of his prophethood, but of his messiahship also.

10

Suffering Messiah?

One major difference between the concepts of the Messiah in the New Testament and the Old Testament is that the New Testament's Christ suffered and died. The Synoptics claim that Jesus predicted his suffering and death and described them as inevitable (Mark 8:31, 9:12, 14:21, 14:49; Matt. 16:21, 17:12, 26:24, 26:54-56; Luke 9:22, 17:25, 18:31-32, 22:15, 22:37, 24:26, 24:46). John (19:24, 19:28) mentions two instances in which Jesus' suffering is seen as fulfilling prophecies. The Evangelists believed that the Christ had to suffer and die. One account directly links the suffering and death of Jesus to his identity as the Christ. Luke here recounts the story of Jesus' appearance to two of his disciples on Easter day:

> That very day two of them were going to a village named Emmaus, about seven miles from Jerusalem, and they were talking with each other about all these things that had happened. While they were talking and discussing together, Jesus himself drew near and went with them. But their eyes were kept from recognizing him.
> And he said to them, "What is this conversation that you are holding with each other as you walk?" And they stood still, looking sad. Then one of them, named Cleopas, answered him, "Are you the only visitor to Jerusalem who does not know the things that have happened there in these days?" And he said to them, "What things?" And they said to him, "Concerning Jesus of Nazareth, a man who was a prophet mighty in deed and word before God and all the people, and how our chief priests and rulers delivered him up to be condemned to death, and crucified him. But we had hoped that he was the one to redeem Israel. Yes, and besides all this, it is now the third day since these things happened. Moreover, some women of our company amazed us. They were at the tomb early in the morning, and when they did not find his body, they came back saying that they had even seen a vision of angels, who said that he was alive. Some of those who were with us went to the tomb and found it just as the women had said, but him they did not see."
> And he said to them, "O foolish ones, and slow of heart to believe all that the prophets have spoken! Was it not necessary that the Christ should suffer these things and enter into his glory?" And beginning with Moses and all the Prophets, he interpreted to them in all the Scriptures the things concerning himself. (Luke 24:13-27)

Luke (24:46-47) reinforces this message later by making Jesus say:

"Thus it is written, that the Christ should suffer and on the third day rise from the dead, and that repentance and forgiveness of sins should be proclaimed in his name to all nations, beginning from Jerusalem." Like other prophecies that the Gospels falsely attribute to scripture, this alleged prophecy does not exist in the Old Testament!

Some of those supposed prophecies about the suffering of the Messiah use the title "Son of Man," which is believed to be another designation for the Messiah:

> And taking the twelve, he said to them, "See, we are going up to Jerusalem, and everything that is written about the Son of Man by the prophets will be accomplished. For he will be delivered over to the Gentiles and will be mocked and shamefully treated and spit upon. (Luke 18:31-32)

However, the title "Son of Man" has nothing to do with the Messiah. As I have concluded elsewhere, any use of this title in the Gospels as a synonym to "Christ" is the "result of the combination of the facts that Jesus used this term frequently to refer to himself, the Evangelists' belief that Jesus was the Messiah, and their influence by a certain interpretation of Daniel 7:13." In most of its uses, this expression did not have any Messianic function, as it was not a Jewish designation for the Messiah. By frequently using this phrase periphrastically, Jesus stressed his human nature and rejected claims about his divinity that had either already started to circulate or, more likely, he expected to appear at some point after him (Fatoohi, 2007: 278-286).

Judaism actually never knew of a suffering or resurrected Messiah. The Messiah was expected to redeem Israel and reinstate the long-gone kingdom. He was not supposed to be tortured and die on the cross in humiliation. Jesus' crucifixion is a contradiction to the Jewish concept of the Messiah. One passage in John even suggests that the Messiah of the Jewish scripture was supposed to stay forever after he comes, as a crowd told Jesus: "We have heard from the Law that the Christ remains forever. How can you say that the Son of Man must be lifted up? Who is this Son of Man?" (John 12:34). The New Testament authors repositioned the cross experience and the following resurrection as a fulfillment of messianic expectations (Theissen & Merz, 1999: 553). What was *not supposed to happen* yet did happen to the Messiah was recast to be what *had to happen*. Reality could not be changed or disputed; Jesus did not liberate the Jews or rebuilt their kingdom. His perceived mission, therefore, had to be changed to accommodate and reflect that unexpected reality.

As the Jewish concept of the Messiah is not associated with suffering or resurrection, Jesus could not have been declared as the Christ after his alleged suffering or resurrection. He must have been known as the Christ during his life, as the New Testament says.

The Saved Messiah of the Qur'an

Jesus' suffering in the New Testament is represented by his death on the cross. But the Qur'an rejects the historicity of the crucifixion of Jesus. It states that although the Jews tried to kill Jesus and thought they killed him, it was someone else who was mistaken for him, so he was not killed:

> And because of their saying: "We killed the Messiah, Jesus son of Mary, Allah's messenger." They did not kill or crucify him, but it was made to appear so to them. Those who disagree concerning it are in doubt; they have no knowledge of it, but a conjecture they follow; they did not kill him for certain. (4.157) Allah rather raised him up to Himself. Allah is invincible, wise. (4.158)

For a detailed study of the crucifixion, the reader may consult my book *The Mystery of the Crucifixion: The Attempt to Kill Jesus in the Qur'an, the New Testament, and Historical Sources* (Fatoohi, 2008).

The concept of a suffering Messiah was a novelty that Christian writers introduced. It never existed in Judaism. The Qur'an also rejects this concept, because the Qur'anic Messiah never suffered the Passion.

11

Scriptural Messianic Prophecies and the Gospels

Evangelist preaching links some 67 Old Testament passages to Jesus to show that they were fulfilled in his life, thus using these passages as proofs that he is the Messiah. In doing so, these preachers are following in the footpath of the Gospel authors. The latter quote and cite a number of prophecies about the Messiah that they claim are from the scriptures, i.e. the Old Testament. Prophecies from Psalms and Isaiah are particularly used. The use of Psalms, which is attributed to King David, is influenced by the Jewish expectation of the Messiah to be a royal warrior who would restore the kingdom of David. This shows "the high degree of perception on the part of the New Testament community that David's life served as a type of the future Messiah. The true Messiah would be one whose experience paralleled King David's" (Marlow, 2005).

In the previous chapters, we discussed a number of those prophecies, including ones claiming that the Messiah would perform miracles (pp. 66-67) and several others predicting his suffering (p. 75). But almost every one of those alleged prophecies has serious problems. For instance, Luke (22:37) says that Jesus told his disciples the following: "This Scripture must be fulfilled in me: 'And he was numbered with the transgressors.' For what is written about me has its fulfillment." Jesus here quotes Isaiah:

> Therefore I will divide him a portion with the many, and he shall divide the spoil with the strong, because he poured out his soul to death and was numbered with the transgressors; yet he bore the sin of many, and makes intercession for the transgressors. (Isa. 53:12)

The problem is that this Old Testament prophecy talks about Israel not the Messiah!

In this chapter, we will examine five other supposed prophecies found in the Gospel of Matthew before we finish by studying what the Qur'an has to say about this subject.

Old Testament or Matthean Prophecies?

Although all Evangelists linked Jesus to scriptural prophecies, Matthew was particularly keen on doing so. He used as many as thirteen

Old Testament prophecies, or what he claimed to be prophecies, that are supposedly about the Messiah to show that they were fulfilled by events in Jesus' life (Matt. 1:23, 2:6, 2:15, 2:18, 2:23, 3:3, 4:15-16, 8:17, 12:18-21, 13:14-15, 15:8-9, 21:5, 27:9-10):

> Matthew and his audience already believe that Jesus is the messiah. They also believe that God must have been dropping hints about the messiah in the scriptures, especially in the books of the prophets. So Matthew goes back to the scriptures and studies them carefully, looking for clues about Jesus the messiah. For Matthew, the recognition of Jesus as the messiah is the newly revealed key that can unlock the hidden meaning of prophecy. When Matthew finds a prophetic statement that *could* be about Jesus, he tries to match it up with something he already knows — or believes — about Jesus' life. (Miller, 2003: 171-172)

The significance of this observation, Bible scholar Robert Miller stresses, is that "the belief that Jesus was the messiah was the basis for the belief that he was the fulfillment of prophecy. It was not the case that people noticed that Jesus had fulfilled a series of prophecies and so concluded that he must be the messiah." He considers this to be the real reason why Jews who were contemporary to Matthew did not find the proof from prophecy credible: "Matthew's use of prophecy has no persuasive power, and can even look like a deliberate distortion of the scriptures aimed at deceiving those who are uninformed and easily impressed" (Miller, 2003: 172). I agree with Miller's analysis, which is in line with my observation that only a small minority of the Jews believed in Jesus.

The following five examples in Matthew show the problems that such alleged prophecies have:

(1) Born to a Virgin: Matthew states that Mary "was found to be with child from the Holy Spirit" (Matt. 1:18), and that "that which is conceived in her is from the Holy Spirit" (Matt. 1:20). He then has the following quotation from "the prophet": "Behold, the virgin shall conceive and bear a son, and they shall call his name Immanuel (which means, God with us)" (Matt. 1:23). This prophet is Isaiah, and the prophecy Matthew quotes is this: "Therefore the Lord himself will give you a sign. Behold, the virgin shall conceive and bear a son, and shall call his name Immanuel" (Isa. 7:14). However, the original Hebrew text of Isaiah 7:14 does not talk about a virgin! It uses the word *'almah*, which means "young woman," who may or may not be virgin. The word *'almah* does not mean virgin inherently. It is the feminine form of the masculine noun *'elem* which is used in 1 Samuel 17:56 and 20:22. In the Greek translation of the Hebrew Bible, the Septuagint, *'almah* is translated into *parthenos*. The latter means "virgin," but it is also used in the Septuagint for another two Hebrew words for "girl" and "young woman." Matthew does not quote the original Hebrew Bible which talks about a young woman, but he uses the Greek translation which employs a word that is more suggestive of a virgin. Some modern translations of the Bible, such as the *New English Translation (NET)* Bible, translate the Hebrew words accurately as "young woman." The Bible translation used in this book, the *English Standard Version (ESV)* Bible, translates the word in question as "virgin."

The more serious problem in Matthew's use of Isaiah's prophecy is that he takes it completely out of context in order to apply it to Jesus' conception. Around 735 BCE, Rezin, King of Syria, and Pekah, King of the northern kingdom of Israel, formed an alliance against the threat of invasion by the neighboring superpower of Assyria. They wanted Ahaz, King of the southern kingdom of Judea, to join their coalition, but Ahaz was fearful of becoming Assyria's enemy. Rezin and Pekah then sent their armies to depose Ahaz and install a new king who would join their alliance. Ahaz thought of allying himself with Assyria to seek its powerful protection against Rezin and Pekah's advancing armies toward Jerusalem. God sent prophet Isaiah to ally Ahaz's fears and give him a sign: a young woman will give birth to a boy called Immanuel, and before this boy is old enough to differentiate between right and wrong, the lands of Rezin and Pekah would be destroyed:

> Therefore the Lord himself will give you a sign. Behold, the virgin shall conceive and bear a son, and shall call his name Immanuel. He shall eat curds and honey when he knows how to refuse the evil and choose the good. For before the boy knows how to refuse the evil and choose the good, the land whose two kings you dread will be deserted. (Isa. 7:14-16)

The text goes on to talk about events that would follow.

Matthew has completely misused Isaiah's prophecy in applying it to Jesus' birth. **First**, there was nothing special or miraculous about the conception or birth that Isaiah described. **Second**, the birth was not itself significant, as it was only a sign to Ahaz about future events. **Third**, that birth would be a sign only if it happened during Ahaz's life. **Fourth**, while Isaiah talked about a child called Immanuel (Isa. 7:14, 8:8), Jesus is never called "Immanuel" anywhere in the New Testament. The context of Isaiah's prophecy could not be clearer, so Matthew must have consciously decided to take the prophecy out of its context to apply it to Jesus.

(2) Born in Bethlehem: Matthew states that Herod was troubled when he was told by wise men that they had come to visit the newborn "king of the Jews." He gathered the chief priests and scribes and asked them about the birthplace of the Christ:

They told him, "In Bethlehem of Judea, for so it is written by the prophet: 'And you, O Bethlehem, in the land of Judah, are by no means least among the rulers of Judah; for from you shall come a ruler who will shepherd my people Israel.'" (Matt. 2:5-6)

The Old Testament prophecy that Matthew cites here is from Micah 5:2: "But you, O Bethlehem Ephrathah, who are too little to be among the clans of Judah, from you shall come forth for me one who is to be ruler in Israel." This is not exactly how Matthew quotes it! The Old Testament stresses that Bethlehem was a minor town, whereas Matthew's change confirms the exact opposite, stating that Bethlehem is not the least of Judea's towns. Matthew meant to say that Bethlehem cannot be an insignificant town because the Christ himself came out of it.

There has also been disagreement about whether Micah meant Bethlehem the town or a clan. A more serious problem in linking the messianic "ruler" in Micah with Jesus is that the text that surrounds that passage ascribes to this ruler historical feats that Jesus was never involved in. This is a longer quotation that contains Micah's prophecy:

Now muster your troops, O daughter of troops; siege is laid against us; with a rod they strike the judge of Israel on the cheek. But you, O Bethlehem Ephrathah, who are too little to be among the clans of Judah, from you shall come forth for me one who is to be ruler in Israel, whose coming forth is from of old, from ancient days. Therefore he shall give them up until the time when she who is in labor has given birth; then the rest of his brothers shall return to the people of Israel. And he shall stand and shepherd his flock in the strength of the Lord, in the majesty of the name of the Lord his God. And they shall dwell secure, for now he shall be great to the ends of the earth. And he shall be their peace. When the Assyrian comes into our land and treads in our palaces, then we will raise against him seven shepherds and eight princes of men; they shall shepherd the land of Assyria with the sword, and the land of Nimrod at its entrances; and he shall deliver us from the Assyrian when he comes into our land and treads within our border. (Mic. 5:1-6)

This passage was probably believed by Jews to be talking about the Messiah well before the birth of Jesus, but this interpretation cannot be maintained by anyone who identifies the Messiah with Jesus, simply because the descriptions in this passage do not apply to Jesus. The passage talks about a king who would defeat the Assyrians, which is not something Jesus did. In fact, six centuries before the birth of Jesus the Babylonians defeated the Assyrians and destroyed their capital Nineveh, and within three years Assyria ceased to exist as an independent nation. The story of the seven shepherd-rulers also never took place. If the passage above talks about the Messiah, then Jesus cannot be him.

Similarly, if Jesus is the Messiah, then this passage cannot be talking about the Messiah. Matthew not only tampered with Micah's prophecy, but he also wrongly and misleadingly linked it to Jesus.

(3) Coming out of Egypt: Matthew says that Joseph smuggled baby Jesus out of Palestine before Herod could kill him:

> And he rose and took the child and his mother by night and departed to Egypt and remained there until the death of Herod. This was to fulfill what the Lord had spoken by the prophet, "Out of Egypt I called my son." (Matt. 2:14-15)

The Old Testament prophet that Matthew mentions is Hosea, and the supposed prophecy is these words that were spoken to him by God: "When Israel was a child, I loved him, and out of Egypt I called my son" (Hos. 11:1). The problem in Matthew is that this passage is not a prophecy and it signifies a past event that had nothing to do with the Messiah or his birth for Jesus to be claimed to be its fulfillment. The *calling out of Egypt* is something that had happened, not something that the Hosea text was predicting to happen in the future; the passage does not represent a prophecy at all. The term "Israel" denotes the "children of Israel," and the specific event that the passage is talking about is the exodus of the Israelites from Egypt, which happened 12 centuries before the birth of Jesus. In order to use Hosea 11:1 for his purpose, Matthew had to ignore the first part of the passage because it reveals that the "son" denoted the nation of Israel, not Jesus or any other individual:

> When Israel was a child, I loved him, and out of Egypt I called my son. The more they were called, the more they went away; they kept sacrificing to the Baals and burning offerings to idols. Yet it was I who taught Ephraim to walk; I took them up by their arms, but they did not know that I healed them. I led them with cords of kindness, with the bands of love, and I became to them as one who eases the yoke on their jaws, and I bent down to them and fed them. They shall not return to the land of Egypt, but Assyria shall be their king, because they have refused to return to me. (Hos. 11:1-5)

Furthermore, Hosea 11:1 and the passages that follow talk about the Israelites' failure to obey God and His consequent anger at them. There is absolutely nothing that links this text to the Messiah, so no wonder these passages are also missing from Mathew's quotation.

(4) Called a "Nazarene": Matthew claims that the Messiah was going to be called a Nazarene:

> And he rose and took the child and his mother and went to the land of Israel. But when he heard that Archelaus was reigning over Judea in place of his father Herod, he was afraid to go there, and being warned in

a dream he withdrew to the district of Galilee. And he went and lived in a city called Nazareth, that what was spoken by the prophets might be fulfilled: "He shall be called a Nazarene." (Matt. 2:21-23)

Like other prophecies quoted by Matthew, there is a serious problem with this prophecy: it does not occur anywhere in the Old Testament!

It has been suggested that the use of "prophets" instead of "prophet" in the passage above is Matthew's way of indicating that he is giving "a paraphrase of the sense of more than one passage rather than a quotation of a specific verse" (Miller, 2003: 115; also Davies & Allison, 1988: 275). There is no evidence that this is the case, as 2:23 is the only prophecy that Matthew attributes to the unidentified "prophets." Of the remaining 12 alleged prophecies that Matthew quotes, 6 are attributed to prophet Isaiah, 2 to prophet Jeremiah, and 4 to an unidentified "prophet." It is unclear which "prophets" Matthew meant, but there is no evidence that the use of this plural term indicates that Matthew paraphrased more than one Old Testament passage.

(5) Entered Jerusalem: Matthew links Jesus' entry into Jerusalem to a prophecy:

> Now when they drew near to Jerusalem and came to Bethphage, to the Mount of Olives, then Jesus sent two disciples, saying to them, "Go into the village in front of you, and immediately you will find a donkey tied, and a colt with her. Untie them and bring them to me. If anyone says anything to you, you shall say, 'The Lord needs them,' and he will send them at once." This took place to fulfill what was spoken by the prophet, saying, "Say to the daughter of Zion, 'Behold, your king is coming to you, humble, and mounted on a donkey, and on a colt, the foal of a beast of burden.'" The disciples went and did as Jesus had directed them. They brought the donkey and the colt and put on them their cloaks, and he sat on them. Most of the crowd spread their cloaks on the road, and others cut branches from the trees and spread them on the road. And the crowds that went before him and that followed him were shouting, "Hosanna to the Son of David! Blessed is he who comes in the name of the Lord! Hosanna in the highest!" And when he entered Jerusalem, the whole city was stirred up, saying, "Who is this?" And the crowds said, "This is the prophet Jesus, from Nazareth of Galilee." (Matt. 21:1-11)

The prophet that Matthew mentions is Zechariah:

> Rejoice greatly, O daughter of Zion! Shout aloud, O daughter of Jerusalem! Behold, your king is coming to you; righteous and having salvation is he, humble and mounted on a donkey, on a colt, the foal of a donkey. (Zech. 9:9)

The Hebrew text of this Old Testament prophecy talks about one animal which is described twice, but its Greek translation uses "and," mentioning two animals instead. Matthew relied on the Greek translation of the Old Testament so he made Jesus ride on two animals. He had to change the earlier part of the story to make Jesus order his two disciples to bring a donkey and a colt. The fact that Jesus could not have ridden on two animals at the same time did not bother Matthew!

Significantly, the versions of this story in the other three Gospels, which are not influenced by the Zechariah prophecy, are different. According to Mark (11:2, 7) and Luke (19:30, 35), Jesus wanted and rode a colt. John (12:14), on the other hand, states that Jesus found and rode a donkey. This is yet another example on how Matthew *fine-tuned* his Gospel to fulfill Old Testament prophecies.

It is also significant to note that, unlike Matthew, none of the other three Evangelists links Jesus' entry into Jerusalem on a colt to the prophecy in Zechariah, or indeed to any other supposedly Messianic passage. Had they seen any such link, they would not have wasted the great opportunity of mentioning it. This further confirms that Matthew was quite innovative and overzealous in his attempts to use scriptural passages to prove that Jesus was the Messiah.

We should note that the Gospels' scene of Jesus entering Jerusalem is clearly political, and is linked to the wrong portrayal of him as a political, as well as spiritual, leader.

Matthew's fascination with linking events in Jesus' life to alleged Old Testament prophecies aims to show that Jesus was the fulfillment of those prophecies. This link, the Evangelist thought, would strengthen the believers' faith and convince the Jews that Jesus is the awaited Messiah and would make them follow him. Matthew was so keen on pursuing this endeavor that he often distorted and misused Old Testament passages. He changed them and took them out of context to make them fit his purpose. He even made them up!

The fact that the quoted prophecies are forced to seem applicable to their respective parts of the Jesus story makes it highly unlikely that Matthew used those prophecies as a source of inspiration to fabricate the relevant episodes. If Matthew was using his imagination to create history, his keenness on linking Jesus' life to Old Testament prophecies would have made him come up with events that are much easier to match to those prophecies. Yet almost every time he linked an episode in Jesus' life to a Biblical passage the latter had to be taken out of context, changed, and/or clumsily applied. At times, he had to invent convenient prophecies. This means that it is far more likely that the Evangelist was reporting what he believed to be history. He used the Old Testament to provide support for the history he had learned about, believed in, and accordingly reported. He simply wanted Old Testament texts that he thought he could apply to the story which he already knew to give it Christological dimensions. He reported a story that was already in circulation and in which he believed. Whether that tradition is historical or not is, of course, a different matter.

Additionally, the suggestion that Matthew made up the events he reported makes the fulfillment argument which he persistently pursued completely meaningless. Matthew must have genuinely believed in the events he reported to diligently seek reference to these events in the Old Testament to prove that Jesus was the Christ (France, 1979: 120).

The Qur'anic Messiah's prophecy about the "Praised One"

The Messiah of the Qur'an was not a figure whose coming was to signal the end of times, represent the culmination of history, or have any impact of such universal scale. The scriptural eschatological prophecies and expectations that were linked to the Messiah, and consequently to Jesus, could not have been authentic. However, the coming of the Messiah was revealed by God to some prophets before he came. Such a prophecy would have described the Messiah accurately, as a prophet, reformer, and miracle worker, but not as a king or someone whose coming would signal the end of times.

The Gospels present John the Baptist as acting as a forerunner of the Messiah — telling people about his imminent coming. This is what Matthew had to say:

> In those days John the Baptist came preaching in the wilderness of Judea, "Repent, for the kingdom of heaven is at hand." For this is he who was spoken of by the prophet Isaiah when he said, "The voice of one crying in the wilderness: 'Prepare the way of the Lord; make his paths straight.'" (Matt. 3:1-3)

This image of John is implicitly rejected in historical sources and in the Qur'an.

In his book *Antiquities of the Jews* (18.5.2), the Jewish historian Josephus (37-100 CE) describes John as a "good man" who "commanded the Jews to exercise virtue, both as to righteousness towards one another, and piety towards God." Had John been acting as a forerunner of the Messiah, Josephus would have known and reported that. Furthermore, had John played this role, he would have repeatedly named Jesus as the Messiah, which would certainly have made Josephus see him differently and not describe him in such good terms. Josephus was a faithful Jew who, like most Jews of the time, did not believe that Jesus was the Messiah, so he would not have considered as godly a man whose mission was to tell people that Jesus was the Messiah.

The Qur'an also disagrees with the Gospels' portrayal of John. He is presented instead as a prophet, like Jesus. There is no mention of him acting as the forerunner of the Messiah. It is perfectly plausible that God commanded John to confirm that the Messiah is about to come and that it is Jesus. But that is different from saying that John's mission was mainly about delivering this news.

Furthermore, the image of John preaching about "the kingdom of heaven" being "at hand" reflects the Gospels' blend of Jewish and Christian beliefs about the Messiah. As we have already seen, the Messiah was not going to and did not found or restore any kingdom.

Yet the Qur'an quotes a Jesus prophecy about Muhammad because it is a reminder to those who believed in Jesus to believe in Muhammad too. Jesus was sent to confirm the verity of the Torah and to modify some aspects of that law:

> I have come to confirm that which was revealed before me of the Torah, and to make lawful some of that which was forbidden to you. I have come to you with a sign from your Lord, so keep your duty to Allah and obey me. (3.50)

Another important aspect of Jesus' mission was to foretell the coming of Prophet Muhammad:

> And when Jesus son of Mary said: "O Children of Israel! I am a messenger of Allah to you, confirming that which was revealed before me of the Torah, and bringing good news about a messenger who will come after me, whose name is Aḥmad." But when he came to them with clear proofs, they said: "This is clear magic." (61.6)

Four times in the Gospel of John (14:16, 14:26, 15:26, 16:7), Jesus predicts the coming of the *parakletos* (παράκλητος). The latter is also mentioned once in the First Epistle of John (2:1). This Greek term, which is anglicized as "paraclete," and whose use in the Johannine writings is inconsistent and highly ambiguous, has been given a wide range of meanings, including "intercessor," "counselor," and "helper."

Muslim scholars (e.g. As-Saqqā, 1972) have suggested that the paraclete, whose coming Jesus predicted, denotes Muhammad's name. It is likely that *parakletos* in the surviving Johannine manuscripts is a corrupted form of the phonetically very close term *periklytos*. This Greek term means "highly praised," which is the exact meaning of the Arabic name "Muhammad." I have discussed the subject of the paraclete in more detail elsewhere (Fatoohi, 2007: 369-377).

The fact that Jesus spoke about another prophet to come after him is another confirmation that Jesus' appearance was not a climax in history.

An interesting contrast between the New Testament and the Qur'an is that while the former claims that many Old Testament prophecies spoke about the Messiah Jesus, the Qur'an records Jesus' pronouncement of Muhammad's prophethood in one verse only. As we have already seen, almost all of the messianic prophecies that the Evangelists attribute to the Old Testament are false and have nothing to do with Jesus or the Messiah.

Muslim scholars have also tried to link Old Testament prophecies to Prophet Muhammad. One classical study is *Muhammad in the Bible* by professor Abdu Allah Dawud — a Roman Catholic priest who converted to Islam early in the 20th century. Such attempts often employ a degree of speculation. This does not *necessarily* mean that these studies are not credible, but they remain speculative.

The Qur'an portrays Jesus as a great prophet, but it does not present him as an eschatological figure or someone around whom history revolved.

12

The Historical Messiah

I will summarize in this chapter the findings of the book.

The concept of *The Messiah* or *one Messiah* must have originated from divine revelation. It was inspired to one or more of the prophets who were sent to the Israelites. But like many divine revelations, this revelation was tampered with and changed by people over the centuries.

Eager to be liberated from foreign occupation and rebuild the kingdom of King David, the Jews developed the concept of the Messiah to represent the military and nationalist savior *they wanted*. In doing so, they lost critical details of the revealed image of the Messiah that *God wanted*, and they failed to recognize him when he came, which is why they are still waiting for him.

The Christians avoided the Jewish failure to accept that Jesus was the Messiah. But, influenced by descriptions that Judaism had vested on their Messiah, they gave Jesus unhistorical attributes and some of their descriptions of him contradicted how he portrayed himself.

The Qur'an, on the other hand, both identifies the Messiah as Jesus and presents him in his real image, without any human interference with that image. The Qur'anic Messiah represents the concept that was originally revealed by God and which predates any later changes made to it by Jews and Christians.

Changes to the concept of the Messiah over time resulted in the appearance of more than one Messiah in Jewish sources. This development was helped by the fact that the Messiah was not a central concept in early Judaism. It started to gain more prominence after the Jewish kingdoms of Israel and Judea were destroyed and their inhabitants were taken captive. This interest intensified in the second and first centuries BCE and grew even stronger in the first and second centuries CE, leading to two revolts against the Romans.

The Messiah's claimed kingship of the Jews and sonship of King David are both unhistorical. The development of these claims reflects what the Jews wanted the Messiah to be rather than how God described him. These two descriptions are linked, as David was the founder of the kingdom of the nation of Israel.

The Christians inherited these attributes from Judaism and projected them on their Christ. Yet there is nothing in the Gospels to suggest that

Jesus sought any form of political influence. He is presented as a spiritual teacher who even went out of his way to distance himself from the attempt to link him to any political agenda.

The Qur'an also presents Jesus the Messiah as a prophet and religious reformer whose mission was to call people back to the way of God.

The Jewish Messiah is an eschatological figure, coming at the end of times and changing it radically. The Christian Messiah has already come, but Christians adapted the Jewish image by suggesting that the Christ would return in the future to found the Kingdom of God, as opposed to the Jewish concept of an earthly kingdom. This victorious return was the Christian response to the low key life that Jesus lived and the fact that he had little impact on Palestine let alone the world, when all Jews were expecting the Messiah to be a very influential figure who would create a new world order.

But Jesus saw his messiahship as one of confirming the divine messages that had been sent to people through various prophets and reviving the original religion of Abraham and his prophetic sons and grandsons. He was a religious reformer who wanted to bring the Jews, and anyone whom his message would reach, back to God. He did not share the view that his time was a climax of universal events or ushered the end of times. Indeed, there was never such a culmination of events.

Despite the major difference between the Jewish earthly kingdom and the Christian heavenly kingdom of the Messiah, both traditions claimed that the establishment of this kingdom would take place shortly after the coming of the awaited king. Jewish writings state the Messiah would establish this kingdom as soon as he comes, and the New Testament authors also clearly thought that the heavenly kingdom was imminent. If Jesus spoke about the kingdom of God or heaven, then he must have meant by that the universal event that will take place at the end of times when all the dead are brought back to life so that the sinful are sent to hell and the pious are taken to paradise.

Both Jewish and Christian sources agree that the Messiah had a salvational function, but they differ in what they mean by salvation. For the Jews, the Messiah was going to save them from foreign occupation, gather them in the holy land, and establish a lasting, glorious Israel. The Gospels, on the other hand, present Jesus as a spiritual savior. But Paul, whose theology has come to define Christianity, introduced the doctrine of the atonement that claimed that Jesus saved people through his crucifixion and resurrection.

The historical Messiah in the Qur'an led people to salvation by showing them the right way to God, which is what every prophet did.

Jesus was not in any way a special savior.

The Christian Messiah is presented as a suffering Messiah who had to go through the ordeal of the crucifixion. He suffered to save people. This unhistorical image of the Messiah was never part of the image of the Jewish Messiah and is explicitly rejected in the Qur'an.

The Qur'an also implies that the historical Messiah, Jesus, announced publicly his messiahship, and he used his impressive miracles to stress that identity.

Appendix A

The Qur'anic Verses that Mention the Title "Messiah"

The Term *al-Masīḥ* (the Messiah) occurs in the Qur'an eleven times. These are the nine different verses in which the term appears:

When the angels said: "O Mary! Allah gives you the good news of a Word from Him, whose name is the Messiah, Jesus son of Mary, who is illustrious in this world and the hereafter, and who is one of those brought near [to Allah]. (3.45)

And because of their saying: "We killed the Messiah, Jesus son of Mary, Allah's messenger." They did not kill or crucify him, but it was made to appear so to them. Those who disagree concerning it are in doubt thereof; they have no knowledge thereof, but a conjecture they follow; they did not kill him for certain. (4.157)

O People of the Book! Commit no excesses in your religion or utter anything concerning Allah but the truth. The Messiah, Jesus son of Mary, was only a messenger of Allah, His Word that He sent to Mary, and a Spirit from Him [that He sent]. So believe in Allah and His messengers, and do not say "Three." Desist, it is better for you! Allah is one God. Far exalted is He above having offspring. His is all that is in the heavens and all that is on the earth. Allah is sufficient a disposer of affairs. (4.171) The Messiah would never scorn to be a servant to Allah, nor would the angels who are nearest to Allah. As for those who scorn His service and are arrogantly proud, He shall gather them all to Himself to answer. (4.172)

They have indeed disbelieved those who say: "Allah is the Messiah son of Mary." Say [O Muhammad!]: "Who then can do anything against Allah if He had willed to destroy the Messiah son of Mary, his mother, and everyone on earth?" Allah's is the kingdom of the heavens and the earth and all that is between them. He creates what He wills. Allah is able to do all things. (5.17)

Surely they disbelieve those who say: "Allah is the Messiah son of Mary." The Messiah himself said: "O Children of Israel! Worship Allah, my Lord and your Lord. Whoever joins other gods with Allah, for him Allah has forbidden paradise. His abode is the Fire. The evildoers shall have no helpers." (5.72)

The Messiah son of Mary was no other than a messenger before whom [similar] messengers passed away, and his mother was a saintly woman. They used to eat food [like other human beings]. See how We make the revelations clear to them, and see how they are deluded! (5.75)

The Jews say: "'Uzayr is the son of Allah", and the Christians say: "The Messiah is the son of Allah". That is a saying from their mouths, imitating the saying of the disbelievers of old. May Allah fight them! How deluded they are! (9.30) They have taken their rabbis and monks as lords besides Allah, and so they treated the Messiah son of Mary, although they were not commanded to worship other than One God; there is no God save Him. Far exalted is He above their attribution of partners to Him! (9.31)

References

As-Saqqā, A. H. (1972) (In Arabic). *Peraclete: The Name of the Prophet of Islam in the Gospel of Jesus (Peach be upon him) According to the Testimony of John*, Maktabat al-Muti'i: Egypt.

As-Sha'rāwī, M. (1999) (In Arabic). *Mary and the Messiah*, Al-Maktaba al-Tawfiqiyya: Cairo.

Davies, W. D. & Allison, D. C. (1988). *A Critical and Exegetical Commentary on the Gospels According to Saint Matthew, vol. 1: Introduction and Commentary to Matthew*, T. & T. Clark Limited: Edinburgh.

Dawud, A. A. (1994). *Muhammad in the Bible*, The Ministry of Awqaf and Islamic Affairs: Qatar.

Fatoohi, L. (2007). *The Mystery of the Historical Jesus: The Messiah in the Qur'an, the Bible, and Historical Sources*, Luna Plena Publishing: UK.

Fatoohi, L. (2008). *The Mystery of the Crucifixion: The Attempt to Kill Jesus in the Qur'an, the New Testament, and Historical Sources*, Luna Plena Publishing: UK.

France, R. T. (1979). "Herod and the Children of Bethlehem," *Novum Testamentum*, 21, 98-120.

Josephus, F. (1998). *Antiquities of the Jews*, translated by W. Whiston, Thomas Nelson Publishers: Tennessee.

Josephus, F. (1998). *Wars of the Jews*, translated by W. Whiston, Thomas Nelson Publishers: Tennessee.

Marlowe, W. C. (2005). "Messianic Prophecies Fulfilled in the Gospels." A Paper presented at the *2005 Annual Meeting of the Evangelical Theological Society* in Vally Forge.

Martinez, F. G. & Barrera, J. T. (1995). *The People of the Dead Sea Scrolls: Their Writings, Beliefs and Practices*, Brill Academic Publishers: Leiden.

Martinez, F. G. (1996). *The Dead Sea Scrolls Translated: The Qumran Texts in English*, Translated by Wilfred G. E. Watson, Wm. B. Eerdmans Publishing Company: Michigan.

Miller, R. J. (2003). *Born Divine: The Births of Jesus and Other Sons of God*, Polebridge Press, California.

Parrinder, G. (1995). *Jesus in the Qur'an*, Oneworld Publications: Oxford.

Sanders, E. P. (1995). *The Historical Figure of Jesus*, Penguin Books, England.

Theissen, G. & Merz, A. (1999). *The Historical Jesus: A Comprehensive Guide.* SCM Press: London.

Tisdall, W. C. (1905). *The Original Sources of the Qur'an*, Society For Promoting Christian Knowledge: London.

Vermes, G. (2000). *The Changing Faces of Jesus*, Penguin Books: London.

Index of Qur'anic Verses

Index of Biblical Passages

Index of Names and Subjects

The Mystery of the Crucifixion
The Attempt to Kill Jesus in the Qur'an, the New Testament, and Historical Sources

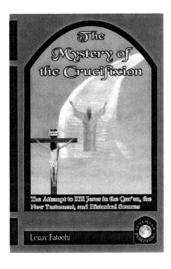

• Flaws of the Gospel accounts of the crucifixion

• Does history really support the crucifixion tradition?

• The Qur'an's explanation of the crucifixion

• The origin of the theology of the cross

• The reality of Jesus' appearances after the crucifixion

Publication Date: November 2008
ISBN: 978-1-906342-04-3
Available from Amazon and other bookstores

Numerous books and articles have been published about the crucifixion. Western studies have focused on the Christian narratives and historical sources, but most of them have completely ignored the Qur'an, which denies that Jesus was crucified. Muslim scholars have also studied the Qur'an's account but mostly in exegetical works that focused on the Qur'an's version of the story, with some comparative references to the Gospel narratives but almost no consideration of historical sources.

This book takes a new approach by considering the crucifixion in the Qur'an, Christian writings, and early historical sources. It discusses the serious flaws in the Gospel accounts and the unreliability of the few non-scriptural sources. The book also challenges common modern alternative readings of the history of that event. One new contribution that this study makes to the literature of the crucifixion is its new interpretation of all related Qur'anic verses. It also presents a coherent explanation of the development of the fictitious story of the crucifixion of Jesus.

The theology of the cross that Paul developed is also examined. The book shows that the doctrine of the atonement conflicts with the Gospel teachings and is refuted in the Qur'an.

The Mystery of the Historical Jesus
The Messiah in the Qur'an, the Bible, and Historical Sources

• Jesus in the Qur'an, Christian writings, and historical sources

• The scriptural Jesus in the light of history

• The life and teachings of the historical Jesus

• The time and places in which Jesus lived

• Jesus and the Jews and the Romans

• The historical Jesus versus the theological one

Publication Date: September 2007
ISBN: 978-1-906342-01-2
Available from Amazon and other bookstores

Jesus remains one of the most studied characters in history. In the two millennia since his birth, countless writers have published numerous books and articles on every aspect of his life, personality, teachings, and environment. Depending on the backgrounds, goals, and trainings of their respective authors, these works relied on the New Testament, other Christian sources, Jewish writings, or other historical sources, or on combinations of these writings. The Qur'an is rarely mentioned, let alone seriously considered, by the mainly Christian authors of these studies. This explicit or implicit neglect reflects a presumed historical worthlessness of the Qur'an.

Muslim scholars have also written extensively about Jesus. Contrary to their Western counterparts, they have studied in detail what the Qur'an and other Islamic sources say about Jesus. The Christian image of Jesus is often cited to be dismissed, usually on the basis of what Islamic sources say, but at times also because of its incoherence and inconsistency. Like Western scholars who have ignored the Qur'an, Muslim writers have shown no interest in independent historical sources.

This book fills a gap in the literature on the historical Jesus by taking the unique approach of considering together the Qur'an, the Gospels, and other religious and historical sources. This genuinely new contribution to the scholarship on the historical Jesus shows that, unlike the New Testament accounts, the Qur'anic image of Jesus is both internally consistent and reconcilable with known history. While showing that our understanding of how the New Testament was formed and our growing knowledge of history confirm that the Christian Jesus is unhistorical, this study makes a strong case for the historicity of the Jesus of the Qur'an.

The Mystery of Israel in Ancient Egypt
The Exodus in the Qur'an, the Old Testament, Archaeological Finds, and Historical Sources

- The Israelites in ancient Egypt
- The Qur'anic and Biblical accounts of the exodus
- Historical problems in the Biblical narrative
- The exodus in archaeological finds
- The exodus in historical sources
- Identifying the Pharaoh of the exodus

Publication Date: December 2008
ISBN: 978-1-906342-03-6
Available from Amazon and other bookstores

Few events in history have fascinated the layperson and the scholar as much as the exodus of the Israelites from ancient Egypt. This phenomenal interest has led to extensive research into scriptural, historical, and archaeological sources. The Qur'an, however, has been completely ignored by Western researchers because of the faith put in the Biblical narrative and the prejudiced view that the Qur'an's account is based on Jewish sources, including the Bible.

This book examines in detail the Biblical narrative of the exodus, showing that it contains a substantial amount of inaccurate and false information. It also shows that the similarities between the Qur'anic exodus and its Biblical counterpart are very limited and the differences between the two scriptures are much greater in number and detail. Particularly significant is the fact that the Qur'an is free of the erroneous and inaccurate Biblical statements that have contributed to the rejection of the historicity of the exodus by many scholars. The book demonstrates that the Qur'anic account is consistent with what we know today from archaeological finds and historical sources. This pioneering study is an attempt to create what might be called "Qur'anic archaeology."

The Prophet Joseph in the Qur'an, the Bible, and History
A new, detailed commentary on the Qur'anic Chapter of Joseph

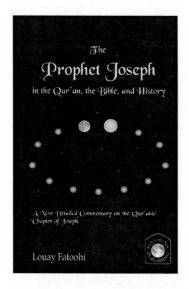

• Modern and comprehensive interpretation of the sūra of Joseph

• Verse by verse analysis and commentary

• Comparative references to classical interpretations

• Comparison between the story in the Qur'an and its Biblical counterpart

• Examination of the historical time and place where Joseph lived

• Explanation of the Qur'an's style in relating history

Publication Date: August 2007
ISBN: 978-1-906342-00-5
Available from Amazon and other bookstores

The Qur'anic sūra (chapter) of Joseph deals almost entirely with the story of this noble Prophet, his brothers, and their father Prophet Jacob. Since the revelation of the Qur'an fourteen centuries ago, there have been numerous attempts to interpret this sūra. The present study is a genuinely new look at the sūra — including careful examination of the historical background of its story and detailed comparison with the corresponding Biblical narrative. While referring to interpretations from classical exegetical works, this book offers new insights into the meanings and magnificence of this Qur'anic text.

The author is not only concerned with analyzing the individual verses; he is equally focused on showing how various verses are interrelated, explicitly and subtly, to form a unique textual unit. He shows particular interest in unveiling subtle references and meanings that are often overlooked or missed by exegetes. Through this comprehensive study, the author elucidates why the Qur'an has always been firmly believed to be a unique book that could have only been inspired by Allah.

CPSIA information can be obtained at www.ICGtesting.com
Printed in the USA
LVOW07s0346030616

491077LV00001BA/68/P